Inside My Head

Head

Contradiction Machine

2016

Authored and completed by

Clyde McCrae Jr.

** * * *** *** ***

Clyde McCrae Jr.

Dedicated to the Memory of My Mother

I would like to give a personal shout-out to my friend Derrick Ball of **"The Derrick Terrell Project"**. Without him, I would be doing none of this.

Please look for my book, "The Testimony of Maurice" coming soon.

LABEL MW

Introduction

This book is somewhat of an updated version of my first book, "Moving Forward". I have included stories from my first book as well as other dated writings that I released to my personal private social media account between the years 2011 and 2016. The reason I've included writings from my first book is because I felt I needed to present those writings in a better light and format. Some of the writings are from many years before 2011 and some are from the date that I released them to be read by the public. In some of the writings I'm not particularly proud of the content, but others, I am very proud of what I've written. These writings are all about growth to me. I write about my own personal experiences in every word. The story "My Father's Enemies" is only *based* on a true story. Every other writing is exactly how it happened within my life. I write about my family a lot. I write about my beloved late mother and how much she meant to me in spite of her questionable parenting tactics. I include writings about my siblings as well. Some are even written to my siblings. I give advice to those who are walking down the same path that I did. I write about how God carried me through all I went through whether I knew He was there with me or not. I realize now that I have only lived as long as I have because God has had a plan for me the whole time. There are a lot of contradictions in this book and I am well aware of them. What some would call "contradictions" I would simply call "growth". I have grown in almost every aspect of my life, from my relationship with my lovely wife, Sherri, to my relationship with God Almighty. I am truly thankful to even be able to offer you this trip...Inside My Head. Enjoy.

Actually written so that generations of my offspring will know me forever. While it is true that I, Clyde McCrae Jr, cannot and will not live forever, these words will in fact live "forever". This book is my gift to you. I wrote and built it myself. May you never forget me.

(MF): Denotes the writing is also in the book "Moving Forward".

<u>Table of Contents</u>

2011

February 11, 2011 4:42 PM

Goodbye Daddy, I will miss you until the day I die.

February 16, 2011 7:40 AM

For years now, I've been asking The Lord for signs that HE is still in my life. I've spent the last 8 years denouncing God. In spite of this, He still fills my heart with the strength to handle all that is thrown my way. I have given all of my pain and pressure to The Lord and now all I feel is divine relief. The Lord has welcomed me back with opened arms. GOD IS GOOD!!!

September 5, 2011 7:49 AM

Just because you are someone's "boss" at work doesn't make you better than them. Some people need to realize that.

September 25,2011 7:03 AM

I need strength. Not the kind of strength that you use to lift weights or run fast, but the kind of strength that you need to stop yourself from crying when it's all you want to do. The kind of strength that you use to brush yourself off and keep going although it seems so hopeless. The strength to carry my entire family on my back and forget my own problems and focus solely on theirs. The strength to not think of my imprisoned brother as "out of sight-out of mind" just because he's never coming home like everyone else thinks of him. The strength to forgive my family for doing that. Strength to keep my head up as I watch all of my children struggle to honestly survive in this world of poverty, crime and what I recognize as hopelessness from my own childhood. As my family falls, I will be the one to remain standing to help you all back up. All of this takes more strength than I have at this moment, I can tell that by the tear in my eye right now. I need strength. *P.S. MY LOVE HAS NO CONDITIONS.*

October 31,2011 8:47 AM

We grew up here. We did the weed smoking, the drinking every day, the selling drugs, the gun toting, the frequenting the County Jail, the unnecessary violence. We were brutalized and disrespected by the police regularly, whether warranted or not. We did the "Rated R" thing also. The lost souls who are out here doing these things now are just the next generation to be trapped by this foolishness. Even the very poor judge each other by what we have materialistically which seems ridiculous looking at it from a 40-year-old's eyes. I'm afraid. I'm not afraid for me. I can take care of me just fine. I'm afraid for my son, my daughter and my cousins who are merely imitating their atmospheres. It is almost impossible to "do the right thing" when you are surrounded by so much wrong. This is a wrong that is disguised as "the only way". We can hold "Stop the Violence" rally's all day every day but they won't stop anything. We can pray all day every day but it just keeps happening. It appears hopeless. Risking jail and death for basically nothing was popular when we grew up and it seems as if this cycle will never end. It is, in fact, getting worse. I don't know about you guys, but I'm afraid.

November 24, 2011 6:56 AM

Although we've lost a bunch of family and friends this year, I'm so very thankful for those who are still here. I am thankful for my beautiful, strong wife every day but especially today. I am thankful to have a job with hard working folks who are just like me. We are doing all we can to make ends meet while at the same time taking care of our friends and family to the best of our abilities. He's going to think this is "gay" but I am truly thankful for my son, CJ (Clyde III). It's not too often a father raises a boy to become his best friend. Happy Thanksgiving friends!

November 28, 2011 6:03 PM

Trust me when I tell you this, I love you more than Jesus ever could. Give me a cross and I'll prove it!

December 10, 2011 7:13 AM

Being an out of control slut should be against the law. What is more valuable than a woman who has vagina control? Nothing! Men *want* to get into your pants. That's no secret. Knowing that, why give them the *only* thing you have that they can't get from somewhere or someone else? Sure they can go have sex with someone else's vagina but it's not yours. Have some self-respect young

9

ladies. What you are in possession of can either make a man respect you or cause him to think of you as worthless and easy. If he leaves you alone because you won't have sex with him then he was going to leave you alone *after* you had sex with him. I realize "loving" someone can make you do foolish things but if you have sex with someone just to hold on to them then you have self-esteem issues that you should probably address. Having sex with you should be something a man earns through loyalty, decency and patience. Never underestimate your own value. Make sure the knucklehead you're going to spread your legs to sees you as a queen and not just a conquest! Humans have the ability to say one thing yet feel another way. Know the difference for your future's sake. Believe me when I tell you, respectable women are envied by other women and respected by men.

<u>2012</u>

January 26, 2012 2:44 PM

I find it hilarious when I see a bad ass little kid running from their parent. It's even funnier when the parent tries to catch them. Sometimes I'll hear the parent start counting all loud and shit. "One, two, three..." Sometimes they yell out empty threats between the numbers. "One, you're gonna get your ass whooped. Two, I'm gonna take you to the car. Three... Does that EVER work? Man, my kid would run from me *once*! Bad ass kids crack me up. If you go to YouTube and put in "bad ass kid" you'll be cracking up.

February 5, 2012 7:19 AM

Happy Anniversary! Anytime I think God has given up on me I am reminded that it's not true by your presence. The unconditional love you have shown me all of these years has kept my heart beating. You deserve so much more than I'll ever be able to give you and for that I'm sorry. What I do have will be yours until I take my last breath. My honor, my admiration, my complete loyalty, my total respect, my love, and if you ever needed for it, my life. THERE IS NO CLYDE WITHOUT SHERRI. There *never* could be. I adore you with all that is me.

February 9, 2012 5:56 PM

Bitches love to not work all year and then, at income tax time, sell their kids to have money for a month. It's the one month that they don't sell their food stamps. It's just true. I have no opinion on it. It's just what bitches love to do.

Mar 06, 2012 9:33 AM

My words are often somber because they are derived from a place inside of me that has never seen any kind of light. We all have our personal issues. My own personal issues weigh heavy on my entire aura. I hate just sitting around waiting to die. I have lived my whole life on the premise that laughter covers pain. It's like painting rust. As the paint wears off you'll notice that the rust has just gotten worse. Perhaps every negative thing in my life is my own fault. Perhaps I've already hurt too many souls to expect my own to be happy. I have always been self-destructive. Perhaps I am merely reaping what I have sown. For an entire life of wasted potential and hurting the innocent I wake up every morning and take my punishment like a man. The punishment of my terrible past controlling my hopeless future. Still though, I laugh.

Apr 04, 2012 6:05 PM

I know this from my own experiences, in most cases, whatever your child sees you doing, he/she will do. Whatever your child hears you saying, he/she will say. You cannot raise your children on the premise of "Do as I say, not as I do". That doesn't work. Right now, if you have children, you are leading them by example. If you smoke weed all of the time, they will smoke weed. If you drink all of the time, they will drink. If your daughter sees *you* being a slut, how is she supposed to see anything wrong with it? If your son knows you sell drugs instead of working for a living, how is he supposed to truly believe that there is another way. I myself grew up without any kind of real male role model so I made a lot of mistakes learning on the job as a father. Even though I've learned a lot over all of these years, I still haven't figured out what truly works. But I can sit here like an expert and tell you what *doesn't* work. Whatever you do, they do. And sometimes they do even more. Props to all the fathers out there *really* trying to pay your child support. *Really* trying to be there. *Really* trying to be a productive member of society. Your children are noticing.

Apr 15, 2012 7:27 AM (MF)

<u>My Father's Enemies</u>

My father refused to go with the flow. He blamed "white" America for all of his plights and battled the so-called oppression brought on by "white" America and he lost every time. I watched him hate an enemy that didn't exist.

An extremely dark, tall, thin, yet physically strong man, my father had serious chips on his shoulders. He quit school in the sixth grade when his father died and went to work to help support his family. In 1957 in Alabama all that a black, uneducated man could do for work was to use his back to make a white man's life easier. My father watched his 6 brothers and sisters be persecuted and disrespected for the way they looked when they were born. He watched his family suffer through hunger and anguish just for lack of opportunity. His father had died when he was young and being the oldest child he felt the burdens of his whole family all of the time. He could see that their lives were different from the folks he worked for and he blamed all white people for any and everything that was wrong in his and his family's lives.

I realized how confused my father was one day when I asked him, "If you hate white people so much why is my mother white?" His reply literally opened my eyes to my father's corrupted thoughts. He said, "I had children with a white woman to piss white people off." After he said this a thousand thoughts came into my mind. It sounded to me as if he was saying that I myself am just a product of his hate. I wanted to know if he hated half of me so I asked him. He said, "When I look at you I don't see black or white I see my son." This statement stuck with me for many years as I watched my father become a victim of self-destruction by his choice to act on misplaced hatred.

I would sit and listen to my father and his friends talk about white people as if every white person in America were against them. These words were imbedded in my impressionable mind for many years. After hearing this talk all of my childhood, I found myself questioning every single white person's motive.

I would walk by a car with a white person in it and I would hear their doors lock. As a young teen I would walk up to a white person's door selling candy and the person on the other side would just yell through the door that he or she was not interested. I had a white friend who invited me to stay the night at his house and when I got there I was on my way back home after about a half an hour. My mother left me with her best friend's brother when I was about five or six years old and he and his friend thought it would be fun to take me into their basement and hang me with a rope from a water pipe. All of these things and much more would be the water for the seeds of my own inherited hatred of white people.

When I became an adult, I watched my father become a crack addict. He even blamed that on white people. He said that if "the white man" did not push crack into our neighborhoods then he would not have this addiction. I must admit, for a few years I bought into this deranged theory. For a while I was even ashamed to admit my own mother was white. I was bitter, confused and vengeful just like my father. I hated half of myself and half of my family. My father sat back and watched as I steam rolled my way through a life of pure hell. My father sat back and watched a product of his thinking fail repeatedly. He would congratulate me on things like selling a bunch of crack or beating a case. Whenever I would show defiance towards authority in any way he would act like a father would act if his child had been accepted into a major college. He would even join me in some of my ignorant behavior. Ironically, his joining me in this behavior would be the light that would brighten up a whole other world for me.

One night my father and I were out stealing radios from cars in a white, well-to-do neighborhood. My father carried an old book bag with a screwdriver, crowbar and several other things that thieves need for what they do. We happened upon a car that had things in it that would make breaking into it worth the effort. I stood watch while my father bent down to retrieve the crowbar from the book bag. Suddenly my father fell to the ground while clutching his chest. I did not know it at the time but he was having a heart attack. I asked him what was wrong and he whispered, "I can't breathe." I did not know what to do because we did not drive to where we were at and it was three o'clock in the morning. I just ran up to the nearest house and started banging on the door yelling, "Call an ambulance!" The porch light came on and a white woman about forty years old pulled back the curtain on the door and looked at me. In my mind I thought that the most she would do is call the police which was fine with me. The woman shut curtain and I could hear her unlocking the locks on the door. When the door opened there was a man standing there. I frantically asked him if he would call an ambulance and told him my father was lying in the street barely able to breathe. This man was white, about forty years old and wearing a robe. He told his wife to call an ambulance and then ran out to the street where my father laid. When we got to my father he was not breathing. This white man began to perform CPR on my father. He was pushing on my father's chest but even more astounding to me was the fact that he actually blew into my father's mouth. An ambulance arrived about 15 minutes later although it seemed like hours. They put my father into the back of the ambulance and told me I could ride up front to the hospital. My father died on the way to the hospital.

The next few days for me were the most confusing days of my life. I wondered how could a man who was white care so much about my father's well-being. I had to see this man again.

I went to where my father and I spent our last minutes together and walked up to the same door that I was at a few days ago pleading for help. I knocked on the door and the same woman who looked out of the curtain that fateful night looked out of it again. She did not notice me at first but after I told her who I was she immediately invited me in. She offered me a drink and a seat. She went into another room and I heard her speaking with a man. The same man who cared about my father's life walked into the room. He told me that he was sorry about my father. I thought, "How does he know that my father died?" He told me that not long after we left his street in an ambulance he called the hospital about my father and they told him that he had passed away. This was absolutely amazing to me. I began to softly cry and he sat down beside me and put his arm around me and told me about his own father's fatal heart attack. I felt at peace in the presence of this man but how could I feel this way when this man was white also known as "the enemy"? He asked me to walk with him out to his car. Even then I doubted his motives thinking he just wants me to leave. We walked up to the same car that my father and I were about to break into. He opened the trunk and I saw my father's book bag in it. He reached in and grabbed the book bag and handed it to me. I did not know what to say. I thanked him again and his reply was, "Anytime." He then asked me if I wanted something more to drink but I politely declined. I left this man never to see him again but I left a changed man.

I realized after these events that my father was wrong. My father was wrong about everything and everyone. I taught myself that to judge a man just because of his race would leave me lost in the shallow, confusing world that my father dwelled and ultimately died in. I realized that I had wasted a lot of my life hating instead of living and learning. These days I find myself wishing my father would have lived so that he could learn that his hatred was unnecessary and really unwarranted. I loved my father but he was brainwashed by 1950's and 1960's America. I loved my father in spite of the fact that he attempted to unknowingly brainwash me. I wish that I could let my father know that one white man showed me that "white" America and myself are not half bad.

Apr 23, 2012 7:56 AM

You never really know what someone may be going through. Life can be rough for people. Show some compassion.

May 28, 2012 12:05 PM

Sometimes something as simple as a phone call can make a huge difference for someone. Just being asked, "How are you doing?" and talking to someone who genuinely cares about the answer can add light to depressing darkness. Sometimes people have bad attitudes because they've built a wall around themselves to hide some sort of despair that they are too embarrassed to talk about. Words are the most powerful things we own and fortunately they are free and painless to replace so share some of yours with someone today. When your family gets together today, look around and see who isn't there, get ahold of those people. Look through your phone and call that person you never hear from anymore. Leave a message on someone's Facebook just to ask them how their life is going. Use words to make someone happy today. It's so easy, free and powerful. How can you not do it?

Jul 03, 2012 6:34 PM

I can understand people who get mad at people who are on Welfare when they themselves work their asses off for what they have.

BUT....

Most of the time it is people who have never been on Welfare and really don't know what it's about. First of all, I hear people say shit like, "People on Welfare are having it easy." If you think Welfare is easy then I hope you never have to be proven wrong. I grew up on Welfare back when your mom could stay on Welfare for like 19 years straight. During Reagonomics. Now, I think you can be on it like 36 months or something. Anyway, being on Welfare has a billion down sides including embarrassment, depression, feeling worthless, just to name a few. The only upside is nothing. My mom "raised" four children on about $400 a month for years and years and years. If you see someone with a $600 phone who you know for a fact is on Welfare, you can believe that Welfare had nothing to do with getting that phone. That's called "hitting a lick" and you do that even if you work. That means basically that you came up on it somehow but it certainly wasn't with a Welfare check. The same goes with people in nice cars who are on Welfare. Just drive through any ghetto neighborhood in Canton. How many Bentley's do you see? The streets and parking lots are covered with oil. That shit ain't from "nice" cars leaking oil all day. Nobody buys $1500 rims with a Welfare check. That shit won't even pay all of your bills. Nobody is living it up because they are on Welfare. They are broke every day except like 2 days a month. Some people see these people as lazy and living off of society and perhaps they're right, but what kind of person would *choose* living like that over being able to pay your bills and buy shit that you want by working? It goes beyond lazy into the realm of mental illness. There are people who use Welfare properly and there are those who don't. But that goes for Social Security, Disability, and even student loans. People on Welfare are easy targets because you can tell they're on Welfare because their life is SUCKING!

Jul 14, 2012 8:47 PM

Today I realized that there is a specific group of people who do not get enough credit. I believe they deserve way more credit because of how very rare they are. I've never had to do what they do and I truly doubt I could do it for the amount of time that they dedicate their lives to doing it. For those of you not doing it, imagine this...

You wake up early in the morning after going to bed late, almost every morning. The first thing that enters your mind are your overdue bills. But as important as those late bills are, they are forced to the backburner by the fact that you have children who don't even know that the rent is late so to them you must "act" loving and cheerful. You must feed them and then get them off to daycare or school because you have to be at work soon. Work, where stress is way more abundant than money. After a long day of work, it is time to be a maid and a babysitter. The type of babysitter in which the parents never come home. You must worry about your children who may be ill or dealing with something in school or whatever. They will be demanding your time and energy because you are good at what you do. You finally get to bed just to wake up and do it all over again. You are good at carrying a load that most of us "normal" people would crumble under. You are a warrior in the truest sense. You have no one to help you. No child support for whatever the reason. Even still, you are good and decent to your children. You do all you can to raise them with dignity by leading them by example. You are a single mother. By definition your "duties" are doubled. Also I believe there is a difference between a single mother and some lady with kids. Not all single mothers act right. But to the ones that do, you're a true warrior in my eyes.

Aug 01, 2012 10:05 AM

I speak for those who cannot speak for themselves. I fight for those who cannot fight for themselves. I target Bullies, whether it be a boss or a stranger or a relative or a friend. As long as I'm around, you will never just walk all over us. Respect is earned and not a given. Get behind me and I'll get you there or die trying.

Aug 15, 2012 6:40 PM

SELF CONTROL...When I'm angry it's impossible not to lash out. When my heart is broken it's impossible not to cry. When I'm embarrassed it's impossible not to feel shame. I probably won't die of old age. My demise will most likely be due to my self-destructive addictions, both physical and mental. Those who smoked cigarettes for a long time and have managed to stop doing it for a long time have more self-control than I do. Sometimes I feel like a hypocrite when I tell a kid that he or she is ruining their future with their behavior as I sit there with a lit cigarette in my hand. I see the consequences of my behavior every day in other "older" people who smoke and yet I feel powerless to stop it. Perhaps that's how kids feel about their behavior. I personally saw from a young age that I get addicted easily to things I like. Whether they be good or bad. That's probably the reason I've never tried cocaine or crack. That and the fact that crackheads never looked like they were having too much fun. I would be powerless to stop it. My father was 10 times the man I am and he couldn't even stop it. So I knew crack would eat me up and spit me out into more crack. At least cigarettes won't have me running out of Walmart with a 42-inch TV on my back, desperately running full speed down the street with it. But cigarettes will have me laying in the Cancer Ward of some hospital being a complete burden on whomever loves me the most. These lousy cigarettes. They're the only addiction that I've ever had that totally defeated me. I'm pretty sure it's the only product sold in public stores that's sole purpose is to kill. Even guns have other uses. I would rather have a period than smoke another cigarette. But, I have to go outside now.

Aug 23, 2012 9:29 AM

I'm so tired of politics and politicians. Democrats and Republicans...just shut the fuck up!!!!!!!!

Oct 01, 2012 10:57 AM

Perfect, you weren't. A "good" mother, perhaps not. But you are my friend. You are my shoulder. Although you rarely told me that you loved me, I always knew you did. Although you rarely hugged me, I always felt your protection. I always thought you were the strongest person in the world. But as I stepped into your hospital room and saw you lying there not even looking like my mother, I realized that even you are vulnerable to life's ending. I stood there for about 60 seconds looking down at you and realized that I am not this strong. Although you could not speak and a machine was breathing for you, I felt your overwhelming spirit, and I felt overwhelming grief. More grief than I've ever felt before. I don't want to have to miss you. I don't want your contact in my phone to be no one. I don't want you to go before I do. I'm afraid that I won't be able to handle it. I never told you how much you mean to me and how much I need you in my life. I don't want you to pass on not knowing that I don't blame you for anything negative in my life. I know that was important to you. I would gladly give my own life for you to live long enough to watch my brother walk out of prison but it's not looking like that's going to happen. Your love for him will keep me strong. I will do everything I can to take care of him until and even after he comes home. I will do this for you, Mom. I promise. Today, I feel more pain than I ever have. Today, I am afraid of your presence being gone. Today, I have done what I rarely do, I prayed. No, you weren't the "best" mother, but I know for a fact that you are my best friend. I love you, Momma.

Oct 03, 2012 11:09 AM

I would have thought that this much pain was not humanly possible to deal with. I share my story openly with you because I search for hope in other people. I search for compassion and understanding from not only my family, but my friends. I like and sometimes *need* to see it. I don't know how to deal with such heart wrenching sorrow. How will I ever be able to function normally when my Mother's laugh is no more? I had never really dealt with the loss of a loved one until February 11, 2010 when my father died. This feels cruel and unfair. How can this be permanent? When I call out Mom, I need you to answer. I need you to make me some chili and tell me that everything is going to be alright. I have to pay your bills because you still need them. I hate these useless tears. They do nothing to help. Where will I go? Who will I talk to? What do you do now? Does it ever go away? I'm being forced to say goodbye to you. I feel so helpless. Tomorrow is my Father's birthday. Perhaps he will see my Mom again and feel as if he has received the best gift that he ever could have. The sorrow is numbing.

Oct 15, 2012 10:18 AM

My wife always tells me, "Just count your blessings and be thankful for them." I've never really paid her words any attention feeling like I have no more blessings than anyone else. I've searched for these elusive "personal" blessings to no avail. I was searching for a reason to feel blessed, searching for a part of my life that would make me look up to God and whole-heartedly thank him for a particular blessing. I have felt cursed by God for years. My upbringing, my lack of opportunities and my family as a whole. (Just to name a few "curses") I've recently realized that I do in fact have a major blessing. A blessing that is one no one else has. A blessing that the good Lord could have given to someone else but he gave it to me. I am feeling good about this blessing like I never have before. Without this blessing I would not be here. *Seriously*. This blessing has always helped me catch my balance when I stumbled and picked me up when I fell. This blessing listens to me as well as teaches me. This blessing is all I live for and all I keep going for. This blessing is, in fact, a blessing to other people but it is exclusively *my* blessing that I occasionally share with other people who need to feel the warmth and caring that this blessing provides without wanting anything in return. I hardly deserve such a blessing but because God is good I have it. I call this blessing my wife. My warrior, my heart and my reason. The only way I can explain how someone like her chose someone like me is divine intervention or what some people call a blessing. GOD IS GOOD.

Nov 06, 2012 7:47 AM

To me, *nothing* is more attractive than loyalty.

Nov 21, 2012 5:55 AM

This Holiday Season my thoughts will be with those who are hurting and/or lonely but don't deserve to be. I miss you Momma.

Nov 30, 2012 7:50 AM

Good Lord, it takes so little to make someone in need so happy. These aren't just words. Help someone who is struggling this holiday season. It feels so good. Especially the wonderful single mothers trying to give their children a decent Christmas. If I can prevent one hard working mother from crying on Christmas morning, I'm all in. Show some compassion.

Dec 13, 2012 9:12 PM

Strippers most likely fart at work. I hate when I fart at work and someone comes up to me and I have to start pretending like 'something' stinks but I have no idea where it could be coming from. That's right, maturity at its finest.

December 14, 2012 10:48 PM

It's so sad. I feel so bad for these parents. It really puts Christmas into perspective. It's about so much more than presents and how much money you have. These people could have gifts galore for their children and sadly it won't mean a thing. Their Christmas' are forever sad no matter what. And every other day for that matter. I can't imagine the complete gripping grief they are dealing with. The sense of heart wrenching loss that will never go away. The maniac who did this makes me think that there has to be a Hell because suicide cannot be the end of his suffering and punishment. (Sandy Hook)

_2013_

Jan 09, 2013 12:11 PM

If you are unemployed *and* depressed they just might have something to do with each other. GET A JOB!

Jan 15, 2013 10:41 AM (MF)

How can people be so quick to judge other people in negative ways all the while pretending like mirrors don't exist? None of our struggling asses are perfect or even close to it. Not me, not you, not no one. Commenting negatively on the way someone else is living only gets your own life put under a microscope. Just because someone doesn't comment on your flaws does not mean your own flaws aren't well known. All of us are either broke, sad, in a bad relationship, struggling with an addiction, struggling to pay our bills, having problems with our children, in an abusive relationship, lonely, in physical and/or mental pain or any number of things we try to hide from each other. We all have a past and for some of us we'd like to keep it there because it's not all good. My point is, unless you're talking about that person in the mirror, control what you say. If your words can't be constructive then perhaps you should not put them on here. I'm not talking about anyone in particular but you know if this applies to you and if it does then go stand in front of a mirror and judge and criticize away. I'm sure you'll have plenty to say. Helping someone feels good. Hurting someone makes you look like you need help but are too embarrassed to admit it. Period.

Jan 21, 2013 9:55 PM

I don't blame you folks for disliking President Obama. If that's how you feel, then so be it. I disliked President Bush but I didn't cram it down anyone's throat. What's the point? It's not going to change anything to say you dislike Obama on here. I highly doubt he reads our posts. Who are you talking to? Me? I hope not because I care more about why my dog likes my wife more than me than how much you dislike the president. Obama will be president for a very small amount of time during your life. You'll be OK. Of course I realize everyone is entitled to their opinion, including me.

Jan 24, 2013 7:00 AM

I hear you Momma. I can feel you. I miss you so much.

Feb 04, 2013 10:31 PM (MF)

Dear Sherri, Happy Anniversary to you and Clyde. I know Clyde always thanks you for what you do for him but on this very special day I wanted to take the time to thank you for a few things that you do for me personally. First, I want to thank you for all these years of protection from being hurt and for your unwavering loyalty to me. Although I haven't been broken very often, I have had my moments of gloom and you're always there to embrace me and to heal me. Before Clyde met you I was always on the backburner in his life but I watched and I felt you teach him how to bring me to the forefront with patience and love. And ever since, I have remained there. I have so much compassion and love to give and now he seems to realize that. Thank you for that. With God's help I will continue to keep beating and working hard to keep a smile on Clyde's face. After all, when he is happy, I am healthy. Sometimes I wonder if you ever really understand how truly important you are to me. I don't even think Clyde truly understands. But I do. I *truly* understand from the bottom of me. It is a fact that when you look into Clyde's eyes and tell him that you love him, it is me looking out of his eyes back at you with complete acceptance and need for that love. It is me who absorbs those serene words of obvious truth coming from you straight to me. They make me so strong, so comfortable. It is me who keeps him faithful to you. I will never let him risk making you break me. That would tear me out of him. Just as you protect me, I will see to it that he protects yours. So on this particular anniversary Clyde has allowed me to speak for him. Although you may never see me, please know that the pure love that you feel radiating from him towards you regularly, that is me. The unyielding need to be covered with your presence, that is me. The unlimited protection that he has and will always provide for you, that is me. Clyde always tells you that he loves you, but this time, it is me. Forever bonded to you, Clyde's heart.

Feb 14, 2013 6:46 AM

Happy Valentine's Day to anyone who may be feeling lonely today. Hopefully, at this time next year, this statement won't apply to you. Everybody deserves and needs somebody.

Feb 20, 2013 8:36 PM

It's crazy how the people who I thought meant so much in my life when I was in my twenties, now I hardly ever see. People I probably would have died for are now practically strangers. "Best" friends who I couldn't start my day without, I now live my life without. We have gone our separate ways. I have met and become friends with new people. Sometimes I wonder, for how long. Such is life.

Apr 05, 2013 8:12 PM

All I've ever done my whole life is survive. I wonder if I'll ever just live.

Apr 14, 2013 6:32 PM

1 Corinthians 13:11: When I was a child, I spoke like a child, I thought like a child, I reasoned like a child. When I became a man, I gave up childish ways.

May 02, 2013 6:57 PM

Today will be my worst day...all I'll do is think about you

This will be your first birthday that I'll have to spend without you

No one could ever miss anyone as much as I miss you right now

Every night I tell you that I love you and I know you hear me...you can hear me somehow

You see me when I'm alone crying my heart out for you

When I'm this sad...I can feel you crying for me too

Overwhelming misery is hidden under every smile

Sometimes it's too overwhelming...so I slip into my world of denial

I pretend that you're at home and I can call you if I want to

But reality is always somewhere around handing me the truth

Handing me more tears...more depression...more lumps in my throat

My reality is filled with gloom...leaving little room for hope

I'll never forget how you felt about things or the way that you laughed

I watch videos of you...I listen to tapes...sometimes I live in the past

I write to you all of the time and then at night on my knees...

I read it to you out loud just in case you can't see

Perhaps I'm filled with guilt because I should have treated you better

I should have freed up many more moments...so we could have spent them together

I should have hugged you much much more than I did

I'll regret not doing that for as long as I live

I miss you so much and I hope that I see you again

I'm convinced... it's the only way this misery will end

I talk to other people about you because you and I can't talk to one another

I want the entire world to know just how much I MISS MY MOTHER   **Happy Birthday Momma!**

May 25, 2013 8:58 PM

If they will cheat *with* you...they will most likely cheat *on* you.

Jun 01, 2013 7:40 AM

I love it when someone tries to tell me how to do something that they've never done. It's so educational.

Jun 02, 2013 6:39 PM

I hate when mothers sit in the house while their bad ass kids terrorize the neighborhood. They be like, "Stop destroyin' this house and take your bad asses outside so the public can babysit you."

Jun 10, 2013 8:39 AM

The News says there is a 40% chance of rain but when I look outside it is raining 100%.

Jun 12, 2013 9:41 AM

I don't see how that freak Ariel Castro hid three women in his house for ten years. I find it hard to hide my cat from my landlord for ten minutes.

Jun 16, 2013 10:25 AM

Not every female should wear tights as pants. Remember, tights "hug" not "hide". Act accordingly.

Jun 24, 2013 7:18 PM

Pet peeve: Someone talking to me at the same time that I'm talking to them but neither one of us wants to give up our sentence. I will never give up my sentence!

Jun 28, 2013 5:05 PM

Who gives a shit if Paula Deen said some racist shit 27 years ago or even 27 minutes ago? Black people don't buy her expensive shit anyway. It appears that white people have a bigger problem with what she said then black people do. Hell, most of us black folks had never even heard of her before this nonsense. The bitch apologized. Let's move on people.

Jul 02, 2013 4:57 PM

People who receive public assistance and don't truly need it are a bunch of things, like lazy, irresponsible, pathetic and childish, but they are *not* a bunch of things too, like, financially stable, happy and having fun. The notion that people on welfare are getting enough free money to live comfortably off of it is frankly absurd. They often have an "I'm entitled" attitude which makes them look even more pathetic. When you see a woman pushing one of those double strollers full of kids plus about 3 kids walking behind her you can believe that *any* happiness she shows is forced and artificial. She is broke and miserable and wallowing in her bad decisions and probably 100% of the time she is receiving public assistance. You get what you work for, and if you're too lazy to work, well then you get *that* too. Only the folks in the government itself get enough "free" money to live comfortably off of it.

Jul 02, 2013 5:31 PM

I believe that if George Zimmerman would have seen a "strange" white boy with a hoodie on walking in his neighborhood, he would have shot him too. My feeling is, the only thing making this a racial issue is us.

Jul 05, 2013 9:55 AM

I've never really been good at embracing someone else's sadness. I'm not even good with my own. It's not that I don't care, it's just that I don't possess the mental capabilities to deal with tragedy that affects those I care about. Perhaps this flaw is my own fault. Regardless, it's just the way it is.

Jul 22, 2013 8:31 PM

I'm sooo excited about the Royal baby. I've been waiting on the edge of my seat for this day for like 8 months and it's finally here! I wish that I could go to England and take a royal shit in this baby's lap. I'll bet this baby is so adorable. As Americans there is nothing we should care about more. Two people who mean nothing to us had sex and made a baby who means even less to us. Of course I'm only speaking for myself because it seems as if most of you don't care about this incredible display of the Royal Family expanding. I mean can these people please sing or dance or release a sex tape or do something that dignifies anyone giving a shit about they're new bastard. I have to get a Royal picture of this Royal family so I can make use of my Royal darts.

Jul 26, 2013 7:11 AM

If you are going through something painful and personal and you confide in me about it, I promise to NEVER use it against you no matter what happens between us. REAL TALK.

Jul 30, 2013 9:31 AM

WORDS OF WISDOM FOR ADULTS...

If you're broke all of the time and don't get a paycheck...

GO GET A JOB

If you smoke cigarettes and you never have your own...

GO GET A JOB

If you eat meals that you never pay for...

GO GET A JOB

If you're worried about the police kicking your door in because you sell drugs...

GO GET A JOB

If you're trying to get SSI or Disability when nothing is really wrong with you other than laziness...

GO GET A JOB

If you sit around your house all day...

GO GET A JOB

If you're living off of someone else...

GO GET A JOB

If you're a leech who steals from people...

GO GET A JOB

If you don't have a car...

GO GET A JOB

If your kids do without...

GO GET A JOB

If you're constantly sitting around waiting on something to fall in your lap...

GO GET A JOB

Give up the lame excuses and...

GO GET A JOB

If you have a job and some of these things still apply to you then keep swinging. Never let laziness and sloth keep you down. Try harder. The key word is "*try*". Always try.

If you think you're too good to start off at minimum wage, then you can come to my house and pick up your check. Granted, it will only be a *reality* check but it can be valuable too.

Aug 05, 2013 8:26 AM

I woke up this morning feeling real nostalgic, missing times gone by. Have you ever had a dream that controls your morning because it makes you miss people and times from the past? I often do. I wonder if I've been ignoring my true calling because it sure isn't what I'm doing now. There is no way that I was put here to make a greedy corporation richer. I need to feel fulfilled by helping others. I *need* it. I wonder if it's too late. We'll see.

Aug 08, 2013 7:29 PM

I *hate* when people say "It could be worse". They always neglect to mention how much *better* it could be.

Aug 27, 2013 12:33 PM

I cry for these streets and I fear for my children. I wish there was a way to reach these lost souls and show them that it doesn't have to be this way. We need strong voices to tell them they're making wrong choices. God bless us all.

Aug 30, 2013 8:09 AM

If you've never walked in someone's shoes, please don't pretend to be an expert on what they're going through. That makes you seem silly and ignorant.

Aug 30, 2013 10:12 AM

If you like to read...

Do you really know what it's like to feel so absolutely hopeless about your future that you can't even picture your future? To be 20 years old and be all but sure you won't see 30 years old anyway so it doesn't matter what you do, who you hurt, or if you go to prison? Do you *really* know, or do you just assume that you do?

School seems pointless to you. How can learning Language Arts help stop somebody from shooting at you for basically no reason? Do you not understand the power of a negative role model? Remember, the apple doesn't fall far from the tree. Do you live in a world where violence is glorified and accepted? A world where love and peace and hope have no place and are considered "soft" for whatever reason? Do you *really* know? What can we offer these young people besides useless words? They need tangible things to raise their hope. They need hope, but hope isn't sold anywhere. Hope is a state of mind that needs to be nourished and sustained through situations that call for nothing but giving up. If there seems to be no hope in someone's life, then by definition they will feel their life is hopeless. I am not one to make excuses for anyone. But I am also not one to confuse a "reason" with an "excuse". The "*powers that be*" have no real answers because to them these young people are just cancers on society. They feel as if the hopelessness and despair some of our children feel daily is self-inflicted. And that's because they don't know. Do you? Do you know what it's like to see the "American Dream" on TV and then walk outside and feel the wrath of what must be the "American Nightmare"? Do you know what it's like to feel as if you would be better off dead than living such a hopeless existence? Sure, you could say that they should wake up and not feel this way, but those are just useless words. Words without actions are as useless as a car without an engine. Do you know what it's like to see your dear mother struggle to buy food and pay the rent with her low paying, high stress job? Do you really know? Do you know what it's like to try to pull yourself up out of the hole of poverty and ignorance with no one helping you? To be totally ignorant to things like, "If you stop this behavior and get a real plan for your life you will make things better for your next generation as well as yourself." When I was young, *not one person ever told me that* and therefore I had no way of knowing what it would take to be successful later on in life. I was ignorant to what a plan was. These children don't understand that you can live for today while at the same time plan for tomorrow. Tomorrow is not real to them. Unfortunately, they do not have the faculties to think about 10 or 20 years from now.

Do you *really* know? You might ask, "How can someone just throw they're life away by killing someone else for nothing? The answer is because a life not worth living, will not be lived. It will be abused and wasted. There is a real difference between just existing and really living. The fact of the matter is, the powers that be have the power and they plan on keeping it at any cost. Not one of us can change what they think about our children but we can change what our children think about themselves. And not with just words but by our own actions.

 Do you know what it's like to be in an unyielding cycle of despair? Do you *really* know? Perhaps you don't *really* know because you don't *really* care. It doesn't affect you. But for those of us who are affected by it daily, we will continue to struggle to get better at coming up with a "plan" for our children's futures. Those of us in this struggle will hear you call us lazy and self-deprecating but it is *you* who are ignorant because *you really don't know.*

Sep 02, 2013 7:36 AM

I'll be celebrating Labor Day at work. Something about that just doesn't sound right.

Sep 05, 2013 8:59 PM

If you let your "significant" other cause you to turn against your family, I know for sure that you are ignorant and you have a very limited sense of what true loyalty is. You are doing something that eventually, you will deeply regret.

Sep 13, 2013 8:04 AM

I love saying what everyone else is thinking but doesn't want to say. I've *always* been that dude that will say that shit. Even if it's about myself, I will say that shit. Although I sometimes find myself regretting what I said, I always say that shit again. If I am asked my opinion, I give the unfiltered version *every* time. I try not to hurt feelings but I am an admitted asshole. I think it's in my pedigree.

Sep 17, 2013 7:52 AM

Hey Steelers fans...welcome to the NFL basement. I know you haven't been here very often lately so let us show you around. Please step over all the Browns' quarterbacks' Jerseys. This room used to belong to the Bengals but now it's yours. Let us know if you need anything. Oh yeah...that bucket over there marked..."It doesn't matter this year" is where you can put your 6 titles.

Sep 26, 2013 3:32 PM

I wrote this "short" story many many years ago. I just thought I would share it with you.

My mind habitually convinces my heart that a decade's old feeling of affection as a child towards another child is as new as the first day that I ever felt it. It's a feeling in my soul of needing the companionship of a specific woman so badly although I know that I will never have it and yet it seems that my heart has never stopped needing it. I know that I need it because my mind constantly demands that I dwell on it although this companionship is all but impossible to obtain. Sometimes I feel this woman all around me although she is never there.

I often temporarily convince myself that with major effort a relationship of some sort is still achievable. In no way do I mean a sexual relationship, but more of an asexual affinity.

This is a true story about one of my many ordinary childhood "crushes" but the difference between this particular "crush" and all the rest is that it has stayed fresh for ten years without being renewed by any type of maintained communication with who is now a young lady.

The thing is, if not for my mother's lack of concern for me and my future I almost certainly would have never met this girl and my time in school undoubtedly would have gone a lot smoother and been a lot more productive.

From kindergarten up until mid-fifth grade I attended a school that did not differentiate between the "haves" and the "have-nots". There were no "haves" so I was blind to the fact that I was a societal "have-not". I thrived at this school both academically and socially. My fellow students were, for the most part, African-American, impoverished children just like me, although I was biracial. Residing in this world kept me immune from the harsh reality of an existing world outside of here that, if I were placed into it, would eventually cause me to feel antipathy for my life and would ultimately change me from a kid with great potential into a mistrustful malcontent.

The indifference my mother showed toward what was best for me threw my life right into the middle of that unfamiliar outside world. I was a naive kid unaware that my mother had just taken the first steps in ruining my entire future. I couldn't notice at such a young age that I had been born to a woman that demonstrated chronic idiocy and selfishness.

While in the middle of my fifth grade year, my mother moved me into a different school district. It was a school district that was nothing at all like the one I had just left. Not only by the fact that now I had become the minority racially but also by what would come to be a more significant fact; I had become the minority monetarily. The poverty that had always been there but remained incognito was now standing up and blocking my view of exactly who I really was. I found out quickly that there were "haves" and "have-nots" and unfortunately for me I also found out that I was the latter. This new knowledge would eventually cause me to take my human decency, my positive motivation and my entire life that was to come straight down a path of complete self-destruction.

My new peers quickly helped me develop a type of pride that made me behave confrontationally toward any one of them I saw as even remotely hinting that they were financially and/or domestically "better off" than me. I would let them have decorum over me but I could trump that by showing all of them that ignoring me would result in persistent bullying and intimidation even though I was really nothing like that. Perhaps I had more pride than I should have had under the dire circumstances I was being forced to bear at home. I would never just accept being socially lower than these people and at that young age I began an almost lifelong, pointless battle against the "Haves". My offense would be quick witted, vulgar insults coupled with crude, unwelcomed humor while my defense would be unpredictable physical aggression. I found it almost impossible to ever be my true self but I actually wanted to be accepted by these people at first.

By the time my fifth grade year concluded I had lost all desire to be accepted and I chose to just be noticed. The next school year I entered Junior High. I was bused miles away from home to go to a school where there were even more of the same people I loathed the year before. To me, they were all the same, bar none. My shame and resentment would be even worse from now on. I began to show out in negative ways even more frequently than I did the year before. I didn't care about anyone in that school or what I was supposed to be learning at that school.

Although I was trying to make everyone hate me I was still an adolescent and inevitably I began to pay particular attention to the opposite sex. Of course there were some girls in that school that I liked but they dwelled on a whole different plateau than I did so I would never let them see any positive energy coming from me towards them.

One of my biggest fears that I still have today would prevent me from showing any girl that I may have been even slightly interested in her, and that fear is rejection. With these girls my being rejected would almost certainly be a given. Besides, even if they did accept me as a "boyfriend" I would have to spend all of my time hiding my personal situation from them.

In spite of the rule I had set for myself, there was one girl that caught my eye that I couldn't resist no matter how hard I tried. I cannot say exactly when I began a somewhat unhealthy obsession with her but it was not long after I truly noticed her. She captured my focus and held on to it like no other person I had met up until then or even up until now. I remember her particularly because I've been vividly remembering her throughout my lifetime and up to this very moment. At first, she could not have known how I felt about her but she may have noticed my diffident attitude towards her and only her. Everyone else was fair game to my twisted aggression and only she was completely off limits to it.

This may have been just a minor crush that every youngster goes through but it blossomed into something more serious than that for me. I know this to be true because here I sit a decade later and out of all of the females I've ever met in my life only the thought of her enters my mind and sometimes controls it for a while. My memory of her is so intense that my mind can show me the adult that I all but know she is. I remember her voice, her hair, and her mannerisms clearly.

As the year went on and I got to know her better I would often wish the school day would never end, at least for me and her. In some ways, I was afraid of her because any rejection by her would surely cause me to be an even more psychological wreck than I already was and yet there was no way that I could just ignore her.

So, for the first time since I had switched schools I cautiously began to show real positive interest in this one person. She probably noticed that I liked her because she was the only person, male, female, student or teacher, who was immune from my infamous, callous behavior. After a while, I was sure she knew how I felt although I had never vocally let her know. Every so often she would speak to me in ways that would cause me to convince myself that if I found a way to make "us" happen, she would be willing to give me the attention that I so passionately craved from her. Well, as much attention as a twelve-year-old can crave from another twelve-year-old.

One day she said to me, "Clyde, what are we going to do? Are you just going to drive up to my house and pick me up and go to the movies?" I gave no response to that seemingly sarcastic question but God how I was wishing that I could have just said "yes" and meant it. The only way to make that happen did not exist in this world. Pick her up? What, in my mom's old and junky car? Go to the movies? What, with me never having a dollar to my name and little access to one? Even if I could have gotten the money there was no way that she was meeting my mother or seeing her car.

I would do the most ridiculous things where she was concerned because I couldn't stop myself. I used to cover my face with my hands and look at her through my fingers making sure she did not see me doing it. After a while of this, she saw me alone one day and said, "Clyde, quit staring at me through your fingers." I didn't think she said it in a way of letting me know that I was creeping her out but more in a way of letting me know that she knew what I was up to whenever I covered my face with my hands and sat facing her. I'm not sure if she found it flattering or annoying.

On one of the most memorable days of my childhood she caught me completely off-guard. Her and I was sitting in class talking about something irrelevant when for the first time a brief moment went by in which we stared at each and said no words. Suddenly, out of the blue she uttered the word, "Yes." I wasn't sure what she was talking about until I asked her why she said that and then she said, "You know what I'm talking about." My mouth instantly went completely dry and for a couple of seconds, I was actually dizzy. She was really saying that she liked me enough to want me to be her "boyfriend" even in front of her pretentious friends. This is what I had been longing for. I thought, "Oh my God, what am I going to do!?" "How am I going to respond?" I wanted to speak the letters "O" and "K" so badly that I could literally physically feel it. But just as I was about to pass out, reality set in and I opened my mouth and said...nothing. I turned around and sat down feeling disappointed but at the same time feeling elated. I was disappointed because I knew what had just happened. My overly shameful personal circumstances robbed me of the chance to, for once, be happy since I had moved here. I was briefly elated because the awkward conversation itself let me know that perhaps she thought about me in ways that I never knew she did. She never brought it up again.

As the years went by and we moved into higher grades we were not sitting next to each other all day like we were in the sixth grade so she paid a lot less attention to me. I still judged myself by what I thought her and her friends' standards were. I was not stalking her per se' because I never really bothered her but she was all I thought about. I doubt she ever knew that.

I can remember one day in high school I was trying to fit in with her friends and I had lettered stickers so I stuck the word "JOURNEY" (a rock group from that time) across my "Trapper Keeper" (a notebook from that time). I actually didn't like Journey nor was I even familiar with their music but I knew that some of the people whom I was trying to fit in with liked them. I saw her later on in the day and she looked at my Trapper Keeper and then looked at me and said, "Clyde, you know that you don't like Journey." She said it like she knew it was just a ploy to fit in. She was never mean when she would say things like that to me and she never once since the day I had met her tried to embarrass me in front of anyone. But I found it amazing that she would even notice what I was up to. She didn't know what type of music I liked. She read me perfectly all of the time.

I cannot state with mere words the impact this young lady was having upon me every day. When I came to school the first thing I would do is look over where she stood in the morning with her friends and if she wasn't there I would sometimes make an excuse to go home and this was going on in high school. If she wasn't there, I felt no desire to be there either. For the most part everything was going well, I mean I was obsessed with her and she didn't know it.

Then one day she asked me for a favor. It was not a normal favor like will you scratch my back for me. She asked me if I could get her a marijuana joint. I said that I could and she gave me $5.00. I couldn't wait to get home and get this joint. I knew I could get it because I knew people who smoked it all of the time. On this day though every effort to obtain marijuana I desperately needed would be futile. Sometimes it was like that in the hood, it was just "dry" that day. I could not go to school the next day with nothing so I made a decision that would turn out to be a huge mistake.

I had someone buy me the papers that were used to roll the joint and instead of marijuana I used tobacco. I don't know why I did something so ignorant but I did. Maybe because I was a lost teenager. I couldn't let her down when she asked for something that I should have been able to get for her. Either way, I was going to disappoint her so I decided to prolong the disappointment for as long as I could. Of course after I took it to school the next day and gave it to her I realized I had blown any hope of what was already all but hopeless. The day after that she came to school and treated me as if I had killed her dog.

After that, I can honestly say that she probably hated me. She never spoke to me again. I was heartbroken. Eventually, I quit school and became the failure I was ordained to be. I ran as fast as I could into selling drugs, smoking marijuana, and drinking. Jail had become a second home to me. I was going right down the path that I was supposed to go.

As I reached my mid-twenties I slowed down a lot and began to focus on mine and my child's future. I stopped selling drugs and got a job and suddenly I was a responsible father. I did a lot of damage to my future while I was continuing our family cycle and every once in a while some of it comes back to haunt me. But she never left my mind.

Even up to this day I occasionally dream about her and for a day or so I can't get her off of my mind. Dreaming about her is what makes me long for my youth. I dream about no one else who gives me such feelings. Sometimes thinking about her makes me relive the same focused feelings for her as though we were in school again.

I haven't seen or heard from her in upwards of a decade but she still has a tight grip on my emotions from time to time. No one else on earth has this power over me. It always makes me wonder what might have been if I had not been so very underprivileged. I can barely remember one of her friends from school but I remember her and I cannot help but remember her. My heart and mind won't let me forget her yet. I don't even know if she is still alive. I just accept and hope that she is and I often wonder if she remembers me. I wonder if she is content with her life. But mostly I wonder if she remembers me although my money would go on her being completely in the dark with any memory of Clyde McCrae Jr. I wonder if she remembers that kid that I will never be again.

I probably could find her but why would I? I would be the same guy who needed her but could never have her, the same guy who wouldn't know what to say to her. She probably has a successful husband and beautiful children. Maybe she occasionally dreams about me although I seriously doubt it. I do not understand these feelings and actually I wish I didn't have them because even now they are so very strong and controlling.

I am happy in the relationship that I am in now. A relationship of five years and counting with someone who I feel is my soul mate. I would never do anything to intentionally hurt her. She is beautiful, understanding and caring. I can honestly say that with her is the first time I have ever been in true love. We have almost everything in common and I love her with all of my heart. However, I know I am still in untrue love though. An untrue love that is not ordinary or controllable, an untrue love that will not ever come to fruition, an untrue love for someone who is basically a stranger to me and an untrue love that I wish I could come to terms with. Really, I'm not even sure that this is any form of love, but it sure feels like it and after ten years it is the most powerful love that I have ever experienced for it has lasted for so very long.

I always wonder if I am crazy or are there others going through this. Are there others who feel the same way that I do about someone that they cannot forget and have an unhealthy obsession with? Is having such fervent feelings of needing someone I cannot ever have just a part of my life that I am destined to deal with forever? To be sure, these are contemporary, sharp feelings that are only meant for her. I've had so-called crushes on other girls as a youth and I have been in plenty of relationships since the 6th grade but out of the myriad of women I've met, not one has ever had the impact on my psyche that she has had since the day that I met her. I often dream about certain ladies that were in my life but after a couple of hours I forget them and the dream. But when I awaken having just dreamt about her, I know I am in for at least a couple of days of feelings that are going to absolutely consume me sometimes.

Sep 27, 2013 2:23 PM

I loved my mother so much when I was a kid that I avoided all cracks just to protect her back.

Oct 04, 2013 3:51 PM

Just because you have tears coming down your cheek does not mean it's time to give up. You can and must get back up because it is worth it. Pain is temporary but giving up is forever. Now, force a smile and GET BACK IN THERE!

Oct 05, 2013 10:04 AM

If you're a convicted felon you should be able to get disability. Not even Walmart will hire a convicted felon. We miss out on so many people whom I know for a fact would be good workers because of a mistake they made 5-10 years ago. It's ridiculous and wrong. They've paid their dues so why do they have to keep paying them? You mean to tell me that a person convicted of drug possession 7 years ago can't be trusted to put a can of soup on a shelf? Bullshit! It is but by the grace of God that I myself am not in their shoes.

Oct 16, 2013 9:26 AM (MF)

You're nothing but poison to me. I can remember when we were first introduced when I was 16 years old. You made me feel so grown up at first. That's probably the only reason that I liked you in the first place. Sometimes I can feel you trying to take me from my wife. I can feel you controlling me. I know you represent all that is wrong with society and yet I can't leave you alone. You stink, you're ugly and I can't help but waste my money on you. I often tell my friends and family that I'm done with you but most of them just scoff at me because I've left you alone so many times before just to bring you back into my life to restart your destruction. Well, I'm 42 years old now and I feel like it's now or never with you. I know that *now* is the time to fight you like I never have before. I think about how much I will miss you at first. My missing you will be apparent at first. I could be depressed, anxious, and even physically ill at first. I must find a way to endure these possibilities and get you out of my life, *for good*. I know you won't really care about losing me because you have so many others under your evil control. I've known for years that you mean more to me than I mean to you. The temporary satisfaction that you provide for me every once and a while is far outweighed by the damage you do to me every time I yield to the pressure and put your butt in my mouth. Well, I'm going to once again set a date on which I will attempt to leave you alone. I will once again battle you for my life. I know you will be looking for my most stressful moments to implement yourself back into my life. I'm going to recognize those moments and act accordingly. I'm going to war with you. I will not let you continue to destroy me. I hate you. You and your best friend, the lighter.

Oct 19, 2013 8:03 AM

Sweetest Day... Some irrelevant holiday that retailers invented to get us to buy more of their stupid stuff because we love someone. We already have Valentine's Day in 4 months. We have birthdays, Christmas, anniversaries, child births, graduations and other reasons we go into these greedy stores and spend our hard earned money on crap we don't need. I love my wife more than anything in the world but "Sweetest Day" means absolutely *nothing* to us. Earlier I gently smacked her on the ass and said "Happy Sweetest Day". It was free and effective and I like that combination.

Oct 25, 2013 7:05 AM

Perhaps it's just because I've never done it but I do not understand what could possibly make someone put crack into their body even once. How can you be that bored? Look around at *any* crackhead. Do they look like they're having fun? Is it fun to walk up and down some street looking for *anyone* who wants to have sex with you for money? Is it fun to steal from your friends and family to feed that monster? Maybe when crack first arrived on the scene in the 80's folks could use the excuse of "just experimenting" but these days the "experiment" is over. The word is out now. Smoking crack is not fun. How in the hell does a younger person even *try* crack these days? That's why it's hard for me to feel sorry for someone addicted to crack. Life is hard enough without the heavy burden of a crack addiction mixed in with it. I just don't get it.

Oct 25, 2013 11:59 AM

Sometimes I wish I had me to talk to and confide in.

Nov 07, 2013 5:21 PM (MF)

Relationships that last take a lot of work. Real mental, emotional and physical work. They take forgiveness and understanding. You must know when to talk and when to listen, when to yell and when to whisper, when to embrace and when to avoid. Work in a relationship is *never* finished. It is a cycle of good times and bad times. You must take what you have in common and dwell on it while at the same time understand that we are all different. No two people think the same way about every single thing. Accept their differences and enjoy their similarities. Go through old pictures if you need to be reminded of why you loved them in the first place. I do that often and it works every time. If neither of you cheat or become physically violent then there isn't a problem that true love cannot overcome. If money problems or jealously or outside sources cause your relationship to end, then it wasn't worth giving it your all. Long term relationships are like anything else in life, if you give it your all, how can you fail? Never mistake an argument for the end of your relationship. That would be like cutting off your arm because it is broken. Give it some time and let the million reasons you love them outshine the one or two reasons that you occasionally feel like strangling them. Love sucks sometimes but it is *always* worth fighting for, if the love is true.

Nov 13, 2013 7:16 AM (MF)

My brother Joe went to prison in 1985 for murder. In June of this year he finished his 28th year of incarceration. He was 18 years old when he went and now he is 46 years old. He has about 14 more years to go until he sees the parole board. It's been a rough 28 years and the next 14 years promise to be unpleasant also. Before my mother passed away, her and I took care of him financially. He's not as needy as he could be but he needs things to make it to where he can live in prison safely and be as much of a human being as possible. Since my mother has died the "burden" of my brother has fallen totally on my shoulders. I have two sisters who are just as related to him as I am but they live by the credo, "out of sight...out of mind". I share a lot of the money that my wife and I earn with my brother. My sisters get money, albeit unearned money, but they can't even share a mere $20 with their brother. I totally understand that they don't owe him anything and any interest they show in their brother's well-being would be strictly voluntary. I understand that they don't have much money because they don't like to work for a living but they both know that our beloved mother would want them to help their brother with their unearned money. What is strange to me is the fact that they both claim to love me so much and yet they prove every day that if (God forbid) something happened to where I had to go to prison, they would just ignore me too. They find it easy to communicate with and help other people in prison who are not even their relatives but when it comes to their own flesh and blood, they just don't see the significance of helping him. When my mother passed away both of them sat in my living room and promised that they would help me help our brother because without us, he has absolutely *no one*. As you can imagine, after 28 years of incarceration, any friendships he had out here have long ago become null and void. Unfortunately for him, he cannot be a good friend to anyone. He can only be a "burden". He is a burden that I am willing to bear. He is my brother and I will help him until the day that I die. And even after that I have it set up to where he will have the help he needs until he can walk these streets again, with or without me.

The whole point of this diatribe is to give a shout out to my two wonderful sisters. You two bitches are exactly what a brother would want if he found himself in a situation where he needed your help. You don't suck at all. I know you look at our brother as just a "burden" on you but the true fact of the matter is, you two are the *real* burdens. One of you knows exactly what it's like to live in prison and yet you still can't muster up the effort to help your own brother out. When do you grow up and assume some responsibility about yourselves? When do you stop putting virtual strangers and senseless addictions in front of your own family? When will you keep your promises to help me with our brother? Don't worry, I'm not naïve, I know the answer to all of those questions is a resounding NEVER! You bitches make me ill, and if you're not ashamed of yourselves, then you don't know what you ought to be. If either one of you respond to this, please remember two things before you begin to type, number 1, ask yourself have I lied in *any* part of this post. And number 2, remember who you're talking to.

Nov 17, 2013 7:14 AM (MF)

The other day, I was told by one of my siblings that I pretend to be perfect, like I've never screwed up. Yes, I have made mistakes. I've made some decisions in my past that I'm not particularly proud of. I used to hurt people physically and emotionally with impunity. I didn't always have a job like I should have. I broke the law almost hourly. I should have had a better relationship with my children, *all* of my children. I used to blame every negative thing that I went through on someone else. I used to be cruel to animals. The man you see before you was that young guy whom we always preach to on our posts. I was that young knucklehead who needed to wake up. I drank a *lot*. I went to jail a lot. I treated women like second class citizens. For a lot of my brother's early years in prison, I too ignored him. I was as selfish as selfish can get. I was quite simply, a piece of shit in almost every way. I consistently imitated my atmosphere. I thought I was living how I was supposed to be living. I really did.

But there came a time when maturity and reality woke me up. At this point in my life I would never hurt anyone purposely for just no reason. I can't even imagine not having a job. I don't break any law that would send me to jail. I have reestablished a good relationship with my hard working sons and my wonderful daughter although I still have work to do with them. I have come to realize that I am responsible for my own destiny and I try to leave the past where it belongs, in the past. Thanks to my wife, I have developed a whole new appreciation for animals. I treat women with the respect that they deserve. I realize how important I am to my brother. I am also one of the most giving people you will ever meet.

I realize I will probably never atone for all the wrong I've done. I am not pursuing "perfection". I know that "perfection" is not attainable by anyone. But I can change, and I *have* changed. I chose to change. You see, I know I am nowhere near perfect but I am living proof that if you drop the excuses, ignorance and laziness, you can change too. Although I still screw up from time to time, I don't let it hold me back. I move on and try to do better next time. And to my two sisters whom I love and would give my life for, until you begin to change, I will be right here telling you that your behavior is totally unacceptable. My words to you are out of love and caring, never out of spite. Please forgive me if I hurt your feelings, unfortunately though, I'll probably be hurting them again, because I love you.

Dec 07, 2013 7:20 AM

When I see a dog tied up outside in this weather I wonder if I'm justified in the rage I feel because of what I personally perceive as pure cruelty.

Dec 12, 2013 8:20 PM

I've learned over the years that sometimes all a child really wants for a present is your presence.

Dec 16, 2013 10:40 AM (MF)

Anger... that feeling down deep in your soul that makes you want to ruin someone's whole life. It can and will control you if you let it. It can and will make you say words that you will undoubtedly regret. It will make you act out in ways that are totally out of your character. Anger is *all* about being out of control. He who angers you, controls you. Anger breeds worrying and revenge, two terrible things. I refuse to worry about getting revenge on someone who has angered me. They will not live rent free in my mind. It's not easy to control anger. But it's even harder to fix something you've broken just because you were letting anger control you. Perhaps we can't control being angry, but I know for a fact that we can control how anger makes us act. I think Charles Swindoll said it best..."Life is 10% what happens to us and 90% how we react to it." If you are angry at someone right now, ask yourself, is it controlling your words and actions? If it is then you are out of control and it's up to *you* to dig down deep enough to get that control back. That control is *yours*. Don't just give it away to someone who wants nothing more in the world than to bring you and your spirit down. Sometimes you just have to let it be. Everyone try to have a great day!

Dec 24, 2013 10:16 AM (MF)

To all the hardworking people who had to choose between Christmas presents and your bills, by default you are the folks who have to ignore the "greediness" that this holiday brings and instead you focus on what is *really* important which is healthy loved ones and the gift of being together. Cheers to those with tears in your eyes due to the fact that this Christmas depresses you for whatever reason. Cheers to those who do *all* they can and it still seems as though it's not enough. Your children love you and not for what you can give them but because of what you are *to* them. You are their protector, their healer, their sanctuary from any harm or sadness. Everything that *truly* matters is free. Children love to see their parents happy and true happiness is free and abundant. So smile and give them any materialistic things you can afford to give them but what they really need and want is not sold in any store. It is a gift that God gave you, not to keep, but to share with your loved ones. It's the gift of unconditional love and the feeling of being blessed no matter how much money you have to share. Share your joy, share your time, and most of all share that powerful *free* love that you have inside of you. We *all* have it. Don't let lack of money force you into a world of sadness. Never underestimate the divine power of a wholehearted hug and a heartfelt "I love you". You will smile on Christmas morning because you're going to realize that there is no reason to cry. This holiday is not about how much wrapping paper you needed. It's about realizing how much you yourself are needed by the very people you are afraid of disappointing because you lack the ability to obtain material things that don't really matter. So, if you cry this Christmas, may they be tears of joy because you realize that it is not how many "things" you have that makes a Christmas merry, but rather it is knowing you've spent the whole year giving your children all you had to give, inside and out. Merry Christmas.

Dec 28, 2013 10:43 AM (MF)

I absolutely love being alone. I often tiptoe along that line of being alone and being lonely. I'm not real sure what loneliness truly feels like. Being alone is not forcing itself upon me. I am welcoming it. I will admit, I am very selfish with my time. I'm not into social gatherings anymore. In fact, I never really have been. My wardrobe consists of "work clothes" and one pair of faded jeans that I've had for many many years. I wear those jeans everywhere when I'm not at work. Sometimes I even wear them to work. I wear those jeans, not because I have to, but because they are familiar and comfortable to me. I will sometimes go weeks without going *anywhere* except work. Those are very good weeks. All I need is my TV, my computer, my kitchen and my bathroom. If I didn't have to work, I'd probably stay in my house for the rest of my life with a sign on my door that reads..."No Visitors". I have no idea why I feel this way. I just know that I do and I have felt this way for a long time. I don't like phone calls or company. I don't like visiting people. Again, I have no idea why I am the way I am. One of my greatest fears is that someone who I love takes my behavior personally. I do not mean to hurt feelings or disappoint my friends and family but I can't change this part of my personality. I don't even know where it derives from. I know that I truly enjoy being alone though. Sometimes when I'm alone, I cry. It is something that I need to do. It is a blissful release for me. Sometimes I wonder if finding such pleasure in shutting people out is even healthy. It feels healthy but at the same time it feels like I'm being selfish and wrong. Even Sherri wonders what is wrong with me sometimes. I know she thinks that I am the most boring person she has ever met but she accepts it and always has. She has chosen to "waste" her life away by sitting and watching me "waste" my own away. The only thing is, I am truly happy with it being this way. However, I'm not real sure that she truly is. As I've said, when it comes to this part of my personality, I am very selfish. Fortunately for me, Sherri is as giving as I am selfish.

Dec 31, 2013 3:51 PM

Life is not a competition. Quit comparing how much you've done for each other just because you're arguing. If you give someone a ride somewhere it doesn't mean they have to answer your every beck and call because of it. If someone loans you some money it doesn't mean that you have to empty out your bank account when they need help. Sometimes people just can't help you, no matter what you've done for them in the past. Stop holding it against them. A "favor" is something you do for someone and expect nothing in return. Some people confuse "favors" with "obligations". They confuse "help" with "owing". I understand that if "I scratch your back then you should scratch mine", but I will understand if you need to let your nails grow a little bit first.

<u>2014</u>

Jan 07, 2014 9:56 AM (MF)

As we go through life, unfortunately we run into people who don't like us for whatever reason. It may be something we've done that they perceive as being worthy of their dislike. It may just be the way we walk or laugh or act in general that makes them not like us. Perhaps it's something we've done in our past to them directly. If someone doesn't like me I have the power to stay away from them and not care at all about the way they feel about me. If I've wronged you in the past then there is absolutely nothing I can do to change that except apologize and apologize I truly do. Because of that fact, I can not and will not let your own personal inability to forgive me control even one moment of my life. I don't hold grudges anymore. Life is too short for that. I also don't communicate with grudge holders. I realize that perhaps I've made a mistake or two that requires more than just a mere apology. Those are the mistakes that I must forgive myself for. And I do. Those mistakes are the reasons why I'm consciously becoming a better person. I cannot change the past but I can certainly shape the future. I've chosen to cut any and all life draining negativity out of my life. Be it family, friend or foe, if your perception of me is negative, I will be here living my life and loving my wife while you deal with your "problem" with me all on your own. For me, being forgiven by people is not required. But my being happy is. As long as I continue to laugh more than I cry I will know that God has forgiven me. And when I shower myself in this knowledge, I wash away all negativity deriving from my journey here on earth. And I shower daily. Stay warm.

Jan 11, 2014 8:40 AM

I love when I see a single mother being good to her children. I mean being genuinely good to them. I don't mean spoiling them. I mean mixing love and discipline almost flawlessly. She never puts a man or any outside relationship in front of her children. She has the ability to make her children think nothing is wrong even if she is falling apart inside for whatever reason. She's making her children *want* to be good people. For the last couple of years, I've watched young ladies do this almost every day right before my eyes. Shout outs to Erica, Kelly, Gracie just to name a few of these special mothers. I've watched you stand tall in the face of all adversity and no matter what you were going through, your children came first. I have nothing but the utmost respect for you ladies and all ladies like you. You are appreciated and the essence of true beauty.

Jan 17, 2014 6:56 PM

Nothing in the body is stronger than the heart. The heart is broken so many times throughout a lifetime that any other part of the body would cease to function after so much abuse. The death of our loved ones breaks our hearts, our children break our hearts, our pets' short lifespan breaks our hearts (several times), someone whom you care about betraying you will break your heart. Just watching someone suffer who doesn't deserve it will break your heart. We call it a "break" but it's more of an "infection". It is infected with love. Love can be the best part of life, but it can also cause you to feel worse than *any* physical pain could ever make you feel. It has the power to give you the best times of your life *and* the power to make you want to end your life. It can provide your heart the joy it takes to beat but it can also provide your heart the pain it takes to stop. We grow to love someone yet constantly being well aware of the fact that we are taking a chance. A *huge* chance. It is the very good parts of love that convinces us to take that chance almost every time. Nothing is better than "good" love. Nothing. Love can be so good that it will, all on its own, carry you through most of your life. Love mixed with happiness is frankly euphoric. Love mixed with unhappiness will hurt you in a place that only being asleep can keep you from the intense physical, emotional and mental pain, and that's only if your dreams are in the mood to show you some mercy. When love is "bad", in *any* way, be it death, be it betrayal, when love is bad, nothing is worse. Nothing. Some think that the bad parts of love isn't even called "love". But I believe, as human beings, we need to feel love so badly that we cannot consciously associate it with *anything* bad. No one is immune, not you, not me.

Fortunately for us we live in a culture where, when we need to, we can mix love with God. Without this mixture, most of us wouldn't have a chance against "bad' love. I don't believe that you have to go to church every Sunday to have the privilege to give your broken heart to God and let Him work on it, to let Him heal it every single time it breaks. I have seen this mixture in action and I have personally felt it work. That particular mixture is the only reason I'm here today searching for as much "good" love as I can fit into what's left of my life.

Jan 20, 2014 11:00 AM

I will know for certain that I am taking my life in the right direction when I am able to consistently practice what I preach. Lord knows, it's so easy to stand in front of someone and wholeheartedly preach to them about their negative behavior. But it's difficult to stand in front of a mirror and wholeheartedly do the same thing. I, like *all* of God's children, am a work in progress. The good thing is, I can feel the progress working in my heart.

Jan 22, 2014 7:04 PM

For most of my life I have been one with you. For most of my life every move I've made I've had you in mind. Your ups have been my ups and your downs have been my downs. When you smile, I smile. When you cry, I cry. Sometimes the most dreadful pain I feel is not my own, it's yours. I feel sorrow that is yours and I feel joy that is yours. I feel hope that is yours. Every good thing about me is your doing. For most of my life I have shared everything I am with you. I am addicted to you. You make that easy to be. I'll never understand why you're so good to me. Why me? You make me want to let the world know that I feel lucky every single day. I have been given a blessing that I hardly deserve. I know that. Even when I am stupid enough to speak to you while I'm angry, I still know that.

For most of my life I've known that. I'm putting these intimate words right here on social media because I want everyone to know that. And I want you to know that I fully recognize this blessing. For most of my life you have done everything it took to keep me alive and interested in moving forward. I am me only because you're you. Point blank and period.

Jan 29, 2014 7:52 AM

You have come upon a time in your life where you are fighting to get through each individual day. You have to figure out how to physically hold your tears back because it's a little embarrassing that you have let yourself get to where you are emotionally. It hurts inside. Inside your mind and inside your heart. Even inside your soul. Your heart has been not only broken but literally abused. It is a "human" situation that you are in. We've all been there. Right now you're being tested by life. You will either be amazed at your ability to fight through or you will be disappointed because you let it take you down. Words from someone outside looking in are always appreciated but it is a fact that they don't heal anything. There is really no one on earth who can take your pain away or even make it more manageable. But there is *something* on earth that can help you, and it's called time. Let it work. Don't give up on it. My friend, you are broken. You are broken from the inside out. And you must heal from the inside out. No amount of words will heal this. No amount of hugs will heal this. Only time will. It's really not even time that heals it, it's *you* mixed with time. It's you accepting the fact that you may be in a situation in your life that requires adjusting to what has happened. This is *always* easier said than done. This takes inner strength mixed with enough time to move on from the situation. The loss of a loved one to death, the loss of a job, the betrayal by someone that you were sure loved you, these are things that we all go through. The situation itself is not unique and going through this tunnel of despair may leave you scarred but you will undoubtedly notice when you get to the other side of this tunnel that you are smarter and stronger for having gone through it. You absolutely must "go through it to get through it". It's all on you right now. For every kind and helpful word your loved ones give you, you must couple that with inner faith and the inner belief that what they are saying is true. At this point placing blame is irrelevant and it doesn't help. Dig deep my friend. Find that happiness inside of you. Use it to come back. Use the incredible strength inside of you to hold on and be strong until time and God help bring you through. Your day is coming. You will smile again. You will have purpose again. You will be *you* again. Now, let's get this day started. We have *life* to experience. God bless you my friends.

Feb 05, 2014 8:40 AM (MF)

Some people love to hear negative things that someone else may have said about them behind their back. I *am not* one of those people. If you hear that someone said something behind Clyde's back, then you can trust and believe that he doesn't want to hear about it *at all*. I can't control how other people feel about me and if their view of me is negative, I would prefer never to know it. This goes for home *and* work. I try not to let what comes out of someone else's mouth control me. The only person whose opinion really matters to me loves me way too much to ever stab me in the back and she is my wife. So, I appreciate anyone who "has my back" and feels obligated to tell me what someone who obviously doesn't like me said behind my back but I would appreciate it even more if it stayed "behind my back". It can *never* affect me from there. I can't make everyone whom I come in contact with like me and for the few who don't like me, good luck with that. Your hatred is one-sided because I've already moved on.

Feb 19, 2014 12:39 PM (MF)

I just wanted to write for a few moments about "my" God. Perhaps you and I have different beliefs on what and who "GOD" is. My God does not judge me for my human mistakes. My God has nothing to do with an overzealous judgmental preacher. My God and I do not care about the words of the hypocritical. Spiritually, my God knows exactly where I'm at because he knows exactly where I came from. He is my conscience, he is my memories and he is my sympathy. When I start going in the wrong direction it is *his* hands that grab my shoulders and turn me. I can literally feel that. When I'm angered or hurt by someone else's behavior, it is *his* voice that I hear inside my brain reminding me of the importance of not letting what I cannot control, control me. When I'm sitting in my home all by myself and I feel an overwhelming sensation to smile for reasons not really known by me, that is my God. I do not need to cram my God down anyone else's throat. I am a firm believer in "leading by example" and if my example doesn't sway someone then what they need is outside the realm of my abilities. I can only be responsible for what *I* do. I'm not in any position to take on anyone else's responsibilities. I have plenty of my own. I believe that when I die, I will not be "judged". I will only be welcomed. I believe my God wants me with him and I also believe that I am going to end up right where my God wants me. I'm getting better. And it feels good.

Mar 04, 2014 8:10 PM (MF)

It seems that every day I look into the mirror I see obvious signs of my aging. I've come to the realization that I just may be on the back end of my life. I'm not as strong as I used to be. I'm not as quick witted as I used to be. However, I'm much more forgiving than I used to be. I can control my emotions a lot more than when I was younger. Father time is hard at work on me, both physically and mentally. My hair is thinning, my memory is fading, my moles are becoming more numerous and pronounced. I've lost both of my parents. All things that I do not gracefully welcome. I am in the neighborhood of 50 years old. Fifty damn years old. Although I am currently at an age that I never thought I'd see, I am not happy with "growing old". I am frankly afraid of it. I am weary of the pain and loneliness that comes with being "old". The slow walking, the bad driving, the adult diapers, the dentures, the hearing aids, the living at the doctors, the having to step aside to younger, stronger, more capable men. It is not death itself that I fear, it is the road leading to it. About a year ago a friend of mine at work, John, who is about 75 years old, saw me walking by him (if you've never seen me at work, I walk very quickly no matter what I'm doing) ...anyway, John got my attention and said words to me that affected me more than he could have known. As I watched John's slow walk and looked at his very mature face and work torn hands he said, "Hey

Clyde, I used to walk like that." For some reason, ever since he made that statement to me I've really been contemplating how quickly I am turning into John. A midlife crisis? Perhaps. But I believe that I reached the middle of my life about 10 years ago. If the early death of both of my parents is any indication on when I'll die, I'll see them both much sooner than later. My time on this earth is drawing down. My only solace in this process is that my God has given me time to at least attempt to leave in people's minds thoughts about a man who started out a much worse person than he left this earth as. My God has seen to it that I am a much happier person than I used to be. And my happiness is growing every day. I will be content as long as I am a better person when I leave than when I came. My life's goal is to turn nothing into something, or die trying.

Mar 15, 2014 10:07 AM

Perhaps I'm a somewhat insensitive person but I do not understand the behavior of those of us who seek attention at *any* cost. I mean people who are *always* hurt physically or emotionally or people who make every tough situation about themselves even if it's truly not even about them. They always have that "woe is me" attitude. They think like, "I haven't had any attention for ten minutes so it's time to get some, be it negative or positive." It's hard to feel sympathy for these people when you feel so irritated with them. This is behavior for small children. I completely understand that sometimes we all have moments in our lives where attention from others is not only welcomed but it is necessary. But every day? Every scenario? *Everything* that happens to you must be crammed down someone else's throat? Even worse is when they get angry with you because you just have no more attention to give these people. Perhaps this is a mental thing that they deal with every day. Perhaps they just can't help it. I'm so sorry to say that I just can't help it either and I don't care to participate in the deeds of an "attention seeker". I don't know what to tell these people because I've never been the type of person who all out seeks attention at *any* cost. But from the outside looking in, you need to think before you speak or act. Before you look for outside help in a situation, make sure it doesn't require you yourself to put on you big person pants and handle your business. If you're *always* upset or if you *always* need a pat on the back, I am not the person you want to confide in. Trust me, you'll think I'm an asshole.

Mar 15, 2014 4:55 PM

Part two of my rant deals with delusional people. You know that person who puts other people down about the same things that they themselves do. They make you literally say, "What?!" Some examples: people who won't work talking about people who won't work, promiscuous girls calling other girls whores, someone in a bad relationship talking about someone else's bad relationship and etcetera. Even worse are those people who get on social media and pretend like everything in their lives is just hunky-dory. They pretend like they treat their kids so good when they are so neglectful. They pretend like they have a job when they're just a stripper. *Every* good thing about them requires "pretending". *Every* bad thing about them, they're trying to hide. They have not the ability to "keep it real" because real life embarrasses them so they get on here and tell us the way that they simply wish it was. They have no desire to do what it takes to make their delusions reality so they just force feed us bullshit. What makes it even sadder is that most of the time we all know that they are full of shit. A lazy person who doesn't think that they're lazy is delusional. A selfish person who has convinced themselves that they are not selfish is delusional. We've all heard the phrase, "Those who live in glass houses shouldn't throw stones", well, these people live in glass houses and they're chucking big ass rocks at everyone in sight. I would say that you know who you are or you know if this applies to you but you're delusional so you have no idea. If you're always being asked, "Are you serious right now?", then you should probably check yourself. STOP PRETENDING AND START PRODUCING! Just stop it before someone who has no problem with being blunt slaps you in the face with reality.

Mar 18, 2014 9:59 AM (MF)

Lately, I've been really pondering how certain situations in my life led me to where I am and what I went through to get here. When I was 5 years old my parents were divorced. I don't really remember too much of them being married. After the divorce my mother met a married man and began a relationship with him that would eventually span over 30 years. My mother spent over 30 years being the "other woman". This married man drove truck for a living and inevitably, because of him, my mother would become interested in this occupation. I call it an "occupation" but for her it was no occupation because she made no money doing it. This married man had 10 children of his own and he wasn't making all that much money so my mom would have to be satisfied with just being with him as she helped him earn the money to feed his family while my siblings and I made due with what very little we had to work with. My mom would leave town with this man for weeks or even months at a time, quite frequently. I can clearly remember as far back as 10 years old. *No* one loved their mother more than me. When she would leave town I can vividly remember feeling that my heart was breaking each and every time she left. I would do things like sleep with her pillow or keep something that belonged to her on my person like it was a matter of life or death for me to have it. When she was home I would do anything to keep her there. I thought that if I personally kept the house clean or kept the arguments with my siblings at a minimum or did as good as I could in school it would make her want to stay home. Little did I know, I did not possess the means or the power it would take to make her stay home. No one did, except this married man who obviously felt my mom's children were an afterthought. When my mother left she would sometimes be gone for months at a time and yet she would leave us with *anyone* who would watch us. It didn't matter if we barely knew them. I went through a lot of hell with this plethora of "babysitters" but that's a whole other story. As I said before *no one* loved their mother more than I did and it seemed like the more she neglected me the more I needed her in my life. I can remember helping her carry her things to the truck she was leaving in because I guess my mother thought this would make me feel better but little did she know, it broke my little heart each and every time. I couldn't control my tears as I would help her load her things into the truck and she would kiss me on the forehead and tell me that she loved me. I believed her. I had to believe her. I can remember watching that truck slowly pull off as I stood there wishing I were dead. I remember that clearly because it happened so very often. *Nothing* and *no one* meant more to my mom than this married man. Not her children, not her family, not even her own health. Sick or not she would be there when this married man called. Sometimes I would wonder if she thought about me after they would pull off in that truck and I would watch her in the mirror until I couldn't see her anymore. I used to think, " How can she leave me like this?" I was convinced at that early age that it broke her heart to leave as much as it broke my heart to watch her leave. I would grow to realize that I was alone with my broken heart. I would go to school and all I could do is think about and miss my mother. I would secretly cry when I was alone because I was much too old to be acting the way I was acting. I would get on the school bus hiding my tears. The worst part about going to school back then was leaving the house with my mom at home and then realizing that there is a good chance that when I get home, she won't be there. It would consume my mind. She was all I thought about. This would last even up into my teenage years until finally she thought of a permanent babysitter and shipped me off to a group home for reasons I still don't understand to this day. Going to that group home would catapult me down the wrong path in life. I would begin to search for anything to replace the void left by my mother. It was the loneliest 18 months of my life. She rarely visited me and when it was the weekend and time for a "home visit" my mother would inevitably be out of town and I would have to stay there with the group home staff while all the other kids went on their visits with their families. Those times destroyed a part of me that I will never get back. Those horrible lonely times have the power to make me choke up even today. Even right now. They were some of the worst times of my life. Eventually, my love for my mother would grow into animosity towards "love" itself. To me, all love did was hurt you. I can remember vowing never to love anything or anyone again. I had no idea what real respect was because I had never seen it so I rarely gave it. I was and am the product of years and years of trying to figure out why me? I saw other parents love their children. Why didn't my mother feel that way about me? What was wrong with me? What did I do wrong? I tried daily to "fix" myself for her to make her see how important I was. I tried so hard to make her love me as much as I loved her. It's all I did. It's all I cared about.

Now that I am much older and angels have taken my mother home I realize that there are different kinds of love. Perhaps my mother loved me but didn't really know how to show it. Sometimes I think that when I was a child she thought of me as merely a burden and even if this is true, I loved her dearly. I told her many times that I forgave her for her neglect when I was a child. I could see the remorse in her eyes and hear it in her voice, and it was real. I know for a fact that that time of my life had an impact on my future and probably not a good one but I am in the midst of trying to figure out how to use this and other terrible parts of my life to better myself and maybe even give advice to someone who is going through even part of what I went through. I look for these neglected children and I try to give them words of hope. Words I craved but never got. I try to let them know that any fault due because of how their life is going is not their own. Sadly, I know from my own experience that they may have a wrong idea of what true good love is and no one there to teach and show them what it is. I'm not real sure what my mother's neglect taught me but I know for sure that it did not make me hate her even one iota because one thing that I know for sure is that *NO ONE LOVED THEIR MOTHER MORE THAN ME.* When she passed away I realized that she would be going on the longest trip she had ever been on. Her final one. And at first I couldn't come to terms with it, even at 40 years old. I'm getting better at accepting that she is gone and never coming back. Although the thought of her and the very sad life she led still makes me choke up, I am finally realizing that none of the bad parts of her life were my fault. I made my mother smile often and it is those thoughts that allow me to grieve and move on at the same time.

Mar 24, 2014 11:34 PM (MF)

My eyes are bloodshot, glossy and swollen. I keep sniffing because my nose is running. I need to be alone right now. I need to be with the only person who *truly* understands all that I go through just to keep going. I need to be alone right now. I need to scream at the top of my lungs into my pillow. I need my mouth to involuntarily frown. I need to lash out, not in anger, simply in sorrow. I don't want to make or hear any sound that might interrupt the pathetic sounds of me "feeling sorry for myself". I need to be alone right now. I need to stare off into the blurry distance engulfed in my woeful thoughts. My feelings hurt. No, not even *she* can help me right now, for with her I cannot be alone, and I need to be alone right now. It is not "help" that I need. It is not "words of encouragement" that I need. What I need right now only I myself can provide. I need to cry. I need to cry good, I need to cry hard, and I need to cry loud. It's how I "let it out". It wants, no, it *needs* so badly to come out. The body can only hold so much of this before it has to just let it go. There's no smiling, there's no laughing, there's no pretending. It is the very essence of depression. It is truly a sickness. For me, it is always very temporary. And because it only lasts for a very short time every great once and a while, I feel blessed. It will never completely cease to happen because what sparks these feelings happens to us all, such as an argument, a failure, hearing a song, even a memory.

Sometimes it feels like these feelings will *never* end. Personally, sometimes I wish they would last a little longer than they do. Not because I like them, but because during these episodes, I am at my most creative. That makes them necessary. It's "my" time that I use to let any pain, hurt, heartache or animosity out of my heart. I use it to "reboot" psychologically. Sometimes it even puts me to sleep. I don't know, maybe it's just me. Goodnight.

Mar 26, 2014 5:07 PM

I hate when I see someone waving all emphatically at me and then I start waving back just to realize they were waving at someone behind me. From now on, when someone waves at me I'm going to turn around and "confirm" before I wave back.

Apr 04, 2014 7:57 PM

How do you have a full blown 200 comment argument on social media? LOL! Telling each other's business like you were born enemies. I've learned that during these "arguments" nothing is off limits except, "Don't bring my kids in this!" People join in making it hard to keep up on who's on whose side. Then there's always that person who can barely spell throwing *everything* off. "You on evin got yor kids's in why you ben thoru wefare! Im in colejj and I wirk."

Apr 07, 2014 5:56 AM (MF)

CRACK

You took my father's glaring potential and made complete waste of it. You are taking my sister's beautiful aura and making her a terrible statistic. My best friends, my cousins, my aunts, my uncles, you've touched them all with your horrifying reach that burrows straight from hell. I've got to admit, even though you've never reached me physically, you have certainly reached me personally. Although I have absolutely no respect for you at all, I do have a healthy fear of you. You could *never* get me. You've never gotten me and you'll never get me. It's not because I'm smarter or stronger than everyone else who has succumb to your wickedness, it's simply because I fear you more. I watched you slowly take my father down and if not for you I am positive that he would have been 3 times the man I even wish I was. Witnessing this educated me on the fact that I would be no match for you head to head. You are the very substance of evil and treachery. I have no defense for that other than avoidance. You may smile when you look at the destruction you've caused in my family and take pride in it, but you must look *up* at me because you didn't get me. Today, I live and stand because I rebuked you at every corner you tried to pick me up on. You can *never* get me. I've always known that your worth is not up to par with my life. Even when I felt my life was almost worthless. It's too late for you now. Now, you won't even get a chance to send me to prison. I'm on to you. I know you. I see you. You will never invade my temple with your evil havoc. I've watched what you're capable of by looking into the eyes of people I would die for and seeing their anguish, their cry for help. No matter what words are coming out of their mouths, their eyes are incapable of lying. The only time I've ever seen my father cry, he was battling you, and losing. I see what you're doing to my sister. Unfortunately, all I can do is sit back and watch you ravage her life. She literally asks me for help but you and I both know that I am no threat to you. There is *nothing* more heart-wrenching than walking away from my sister knowing that she is in the fight of her life and *all* I can do is watch and grieve for her.

All my life, I have avoided you and yet all my life you have negatively affected me. I tell you over and over that "you will never get me" but in reality when I see my sister being destroyed by you and I feel her pain like it's my own, I realize that you've already got me. You've had me the whole time. Because I cannot fight you or press charges on you or kill you, all I can do is ask you, before it's too late, please, *please*... let her go.

Apr 10, 2014 8:33 PM (MF)

NOTHING is more important to a man than a loyal woman, a faithful REAL "partner". You don't even think about her cheating on you because that is so far from what your relationship is made of that it just couldn't happen. She does so much for you but falls well short of being a mere pushover. She does it because she loves you and perhaps more importantly, she does it because she wants to. It feels good to have such loyal love set in stone to last years upon years. She would never leave you. Not because of threats and fear but because she genuinely couldn't imagine life without you and that feeling is mutual. She is living proof that at least some of life is dictated by luck. Because sometimes you just look at her without her knowing and realize how incredibly lucky you are to not only have her in your life, but to be the one she chooses to give so much of her precious loyalty to. What an incredible feeling of security and sense of worth. What a wonderful part of life. She would never speak ill of you behind your back. She will blindly defend even your name. It's almost as if she is somehow "forcing" you to love her. This type of woman can easily be taken advantage of by a man who isn't "ready" for what she is bringing to the table. But it would only happen once. She's not the type to treat love like a childish game. She knows her worth and if you want to hold on to her, you'd better know it too. This type of woman *really* "wants" you, but doesn't

really "need" you because she could easily sta
own two feet if you force her to by taking advantage of
her trust. Loyal women should have a national holiday
because not every woman falls into this category and the
ones who do should be placed on a pedestal above the
ones who don't. A loyal good woman is simply better than
one who isn't. Simply...better.

Apr 13, 2014 10:03 AM (MF)

The Past...

The past is a place. It is a place some people will try to
force you to go back to whether you want to or not. Those
who judge us by things we've done in our past have no
idea how far removed from that we truly are. They have
no idea how hard we've fought to improve upon the
casserole of mistakes we may have made. Perhaps these
mistakes never go away but it is a fact that they are
locked away in life's attic and the attic door is sealed shut.
Some people pound on that door, trying to break it down
to not only see what's in there but to lay some validity to
their pure jealously. "Yeah, she's a good mom *now*, but
back in the day she was always in the street." "He's a hard
worker *now* but back in the day all he did was sell drugs."
"She's faithful *now* but back in the day she was a big ass
hoe." "All of a sudden he is a Christian but a few years ago

he would curse his own mother out." "She doesn't want anyone to know that a couple of years ago she was on drugs." These are just some examples of words used by someone who can't deal with you changing your life while theirs remain in childish shambles. These people have never let their past go and all it does is impede upon their present. Then they try to get *you* to live that way. They may say that you think you're "too good" now, and if they say that then they are absolutely correct, we are "too good" for that. We are "too good" to let a dormant past interfere with a brand new present and a hopeful future. We are "too good" to let their negative words rekindle a negative flame that has been not only blown out, but doused, never to be relit. We are "too good" to go where they're trying to take us. There is *nothing* wrong with falling down into the dirt and maybe even staying down for a few moments and then giving it all you have to stand back up and brush yourself off and begin to take your life full steam ahead. The folks you left lying in that dirt will try so hard to pull you back down there because that's easier than trying to stand up themselves. Don't let them do it. Smack their hand off of you and brush the little bit of dirt off that they tried to put on you and live. Live for now. Live for tomorrow. Let the jealous know that no matter what they say about you, no matter how they feel about you, you're much too strong now to ever be pulled back to the place where they choose to dwell... the past.

Apr 14, 2014 8:47 AM (MF)

My Role Model

I can remember as far back as 9 years old Growing up with my best friend, my role model, my older brother. My brother was 4 years older than me and quite big for his age. He was a scary violent teenager whom I admired as a kid. I can remember living in that cesspool Highland Park in the late 70's and watching my brother terrorize almost anyone he would come in contact with. I committed my first burglary with my brother. I was 9 years old and he was 13. It was an apartment in Highland Park. It was a day pretty much like any other day. I would follow my brother around and witness the evil he had inside of him come out almost every day. On this day his victim would be a frail elderly lady. He somehow got into her front door without breaking the lock. When we entered the apartment it was obvious that no one was home. I was so young that all I could do was be terrified of getting caught in this lady's apartment. After a few minutes inside the apartment my brother began to gather some of this lady's things together and place them on a sheet he had laid in her living room. I just stood in the kitchen going through the lady's refrigerator where I found some sort of fudge in a jar. I opened the jar and began to eat it with my fingers while my brother ransacked the apartment. All of a sudden I hear keys jingling at the front door. My brother runs to where I am with a sheet full of this lady's belongings and he stands behind the door waiting on whoever is at the door to come in. As the door began to slowly open I saw her. She had to be 80 years old. As she walked into the apartment my brother jumped from behind the door and clotheslined this poor woman. He hit her so hard that she didn't even know *what* had hit her. She hit the ground with tremendous force and I could feel myself standing there with my eyes as wide open as my mouth but what I didn't notice at the time was the sound coming from my throat. I was screaming at the top of my lungs because I was almost sure I had just seen someone be killed. Suddenly, my brother's voice broke through the paralyzing fear that had taken over my entire psyche. "Come on!", he yelled. He grabbed my shirt and literally pulled me out of the apartment while I continued to stare at his victim having trouble breathing on the floor. When we ran from the apartment my brother reiterated his number one rule to me, " Keep your fuckin' mouth shut!" He had stolen an alarm clock from this lady and I can remember always seeing it in our bedroom and feeling bad because of what it represented to me.

Another time up in Highland Park he had me wait outside of this elderly gentleman's apartment and told me that he was going to go inside the apartment to talk to the old man about something. What you need to understand is that whatever my brother told me to do, I did, without question. I stood outside this man's apartment for about an hour before I saw my brother literally dive out of this man's bedroom window. He looked up at me and yelled, "Patches, Look!" I looked through the window my brother had just shattered by diving through it and I saw the man running toward the window absolutely nude and yelling, "Give me my money back!" I have no idea what went on inside that apartment before my brother dove through the window but my brother didn't seem to care who saw what was going on outside. There were people everywhere watching this. He had stolen the man's money by most likely promising to have sex with him. My brother was 13 years old. We just left there and carried on like nothing had happened.

I followed my brother everywhere he went. Sometimes I would follow him without him knowing I was. If he didn't want me following him he would yell for me to quit following him and I used to do it anyway, kind of like a gnat that won't leave your face alone. He taught me that following him when he didn't want me to would have consequences. One day I was following him and he kept telling me to go away but I just couldn't. I can't understand why I would even want to follow him when all he did was scare me half to death every day. Perhaps it was because he was all I had as far as a role model and father figure. I can remember following him without his permission once too often. He picked up an empty 40-

ounce bottle and threw it as hard as he could on the concrete right in front of me. I can only assume that he thought the bottle would break but it didn't. It bounced off of the concrete and hit me directly in the kneecap, basically destroying my 9-year-old knee. I quickly fell to the ground screaming. My brother ran over to me and without hesitation began to try to force me to get up and walk. There was no way. He left me lay there and then he ran away. I literally crawled to our apartment in agonizing pain. My brother ran away from home that day and not because he was "afraid" that there would be consequences but because he didn't want to have to deal with anyone's "bitching" about it. He was not afraid of my mother. He was not afraid of anyone as far as I could tell. We had no "real" father so all he had to contend with would be my mother whom he would get physical with at the drop of a hat. He was about 13 years old and already bigger than her. I can remember my brother being "locked-up" even more than he was free.

I can sit here and tell you countless stories about the violence my brother inflicted upon the folks and animals in our community but the violence he inflicted upon me personally is what makes me cringe even to this day. My brother would sometimes hit me so hard that he would literally knock me unconscious. He would punch me in my head or anywhere else he felt like hitting me. I could barely walk past him without him physically abusing me in some way. But at night, at night is when he would unleash the monster that I found to be the scariest. He sexually abused me. I will not elaborate on that but I will say that he was a sick child. I hated the darkness because of this. I was too afraid to tell my mother or anyone else because he had threatened to kill everyone if I told anyone. After all the violence I had seen my brother do to people my young mind had no reason to believe he would do no less than kill me and everyone I loved if I told a soul. So I remained silent about it.

As we got older I watched him commit some atrocities against people, even people we knew. He had absolutely no limits to his violence. *No one* was off limits. Eventually in 1985 he killed a man by beating him to death with a tire iron and a wood splitting maul. This act would do him in. I remember the police at our house looking for him and rummaging through things in our house. They took almost all of my brother's belongings. He was "a fugitive" at 18 years old. I remember hearing the police tell my mother that if he didn't turn himself in that there was a good chance he would be killed. He was facing the death penalty and he was considered armed and dangerous, and that's exactly what he was. Eventually, my mother talked him into turning himself in and in June of 1985 my brother was locked up one last time for what would turn out to be a 42-year sentence. The first few years of my brother's life in prison were rough on us all. He was *always* in trouble and fighting. He was in Lucasville State Prison and, as much as I hate to admit it, he belonged there.

Here we are 28 years later and today my brother is a different person. He has matured tremendously. In the last 15 years he has gotten into no trouble at all in prison and he is looking forward to coming home in 2025. He will be 60 years old when he is released. I love my brother in spite of his tremendous abuse of not only me but everyone around him. I look at him as not the same person he was back then. I forgive him. And since my beloved mother passed away a couple of years ago, I am all he has now. I'm sure that watching my brother over all of those years influenced some of my own terrible behavior when I was a young adult but I stopped behaving that way because I had something my brother *never* had and that is a conscience. I was also *very* lucky to have avoided prison or killing anyone. I always feel that, for some reason, God felt as if he should watch over me as I traveled through the valley of death. HE has always helped me avoid the terrible fate that I was all but asking for and doomed to. My survival can *only* be attributed to THE ALMIGHTY. There's no other explanation.

Apr 27, 2014 6:29 AM

Guns, alcohol and hopelessness is a cocktail served up by Satan himself. This cocktail, in the hands of our youth, helps populate our cemeteries and prisons. To our youth, guns are easy to get, alcohol is easy to get and the feeling of hopelessness has always been there. If drugs are thrown into the mix it becomes an Armageddon in our community. This is a battle that has been going on in our communities for generations. "Good vs Evil" perhaps. Evil is a worthy adversary to us all. We must find a way to get our youth off of this battlefield, but how? Some of our naïve yet beautiful friends will bring "religion" up but I can tell you from experience that religion doesn't work on everyone. I wish it did. I really do.

Apr 27, 2014 5:10 PM (MF)

"Me"

Some of us take things out on our mothers simply because we know that there is no one more forgiving than a mother. Sometimes we lash out at them as though they were a stranger on the street. Just think of some of the sacrifices that must be made by a mother. Most fathers can decide to ignore his children and go live his life without them. But most mothers must ignore all temptations to leave and fight through. She must always put her own feelings and life aside to handle anything her children may be going through. She is silent about her own angst because she has no time for falling apart or giving up. She is a person who *never* deserves to be disrespected and yet she takes that too. She takes being judged by how she chose to handle the struggles that come with being a mother. Decisions which involve a choice between self-happiness and the happiness of a child are not always easy decisions to make. I was one who blamed my mother. I blamed her for the way I was living, for the way I was going to be living and even for the bad decisions that I made that really had nothing to do with her. I'm not real sure about exactly how much regret she may have had stored in her heart but I often searched for that regret in an attempt to exploit it. I needed someone to blame. I needed someone to be at fault for my life and she was an easy target. Of course, my screwing up my own life had to be someone else's fault, right? My decision to quit school, my decision to go out breaking the law and going to jail, my decision to have more children than I could afford, my decision to give up on life before it even really started, these decisions I made were her fault, no? Of course they weren't. These were my own decisions and I own them. You see people, we are responsible for our own decisions. Whether they be good ones or bad ones. My mother couldn't go to school for me. She was not with me *one* time when I committed any crime. My mother never ever said to me, " You should have sex without protection and have more children than you can afford." My mother had the ability to feel pride for me and it is my own fault that I rarely made her use that ability. Perhaps my mother owned my world when I was a child and it is a fact that she made some questionable decisions. But when I became an adult I took my world from my mother and began to abuse it *all on my own*. She never made one decision for me when I became an adult. I never asked her for advice one time. I did blame her though. How she must have felt being blamed for things that she had nothing to do with. I was so convinced that everything was her fault that sometimes I cringe at the thought of I may have manipulated her into believing that the behavior I chose to display was because of her. It's regret, and it's too late for me now. It's too late for me to let my mother know that all the blame I tried to place upon her belongs to me. It's too late to let her know that my heart has matured enough for me to see how hard it was for her. I hope you never feel this type of "regret". I hope you still have time to realize that if you are forcing yourself to place "blame", you shouldn't place it upon your mother. After all of this time I have finally learned the name of the person who is truly to blame for my decisions and I call him "Me".

Apr 29, 2014 10:29 AM (MF)

Being biracial means I have never really had true racism in my heart. By definition, it's impossible. My mother was as white as white can get and my father was as black as black can get. However, I must admit that my atmosphere growing up let me know that society considered me as "black". I have been called a "nigger" by white people. Even white people in my own family. This derogatory name being thrown at me personally over the years has geared my mind into accepting that at least to most people around me, I am black. Sometimes I used wonder about myself, "Am I "being" black or am I just "acting" black?" Unfortunately, society sometimes forced me to at least ponder such an irrelevant question. I never could tell because there is no way to just ignore that 50% of my DNA is from a white person. What would it be like if every person in America were my "race"? We'd have to find something besides race to hate each other for, and unfortunately, I'm sure we would. For me personally, I refuse to categorize myself. I'll let society do that. I cannot hate white people because I truly love too many of them. I cannot hate black people because I truly love too many of them. Perhaps being both races makes me neither race, and that's what I'd rather be.

May 03, 2014 7:15 AM

Lonely, and I want to be. Today is my beloved mother's birthday. I miss her so much. Much love my friends.

May 03, 2014 9:52 AM (MF)

I awoke this morning with you on my mind heavily. My wanting to come see you but not knowing where "nowhere" is caused me to become overwhelmed emotionally and so I began to cry uncontrollably. I wondered if you were watching me. Perhaps you were sitting beside me on my bed as I crossed my arms, rocking back and forth, holding myself trying to locate some type of emotional comfort. Perhaps you cried too. I am remembering your smile today and your laughter. Today I will do my best to remember the joyous parts of our relationship. I completely took your presence for granted and I wish I could apologize to you for that. I miss hugging you and I didn't realize at the time how very important those moments would end up being. I was a fool. This morning, I shook with grief and I deserved to. That's my warranted guilt walking around in my mind causing havoc. Every moment that I chose not to spend with you is now coming back to haunt me. Every single moment. I want you to know Momma, I'm still here, wishing you were too. I'm still hurting. I still miss you, and I will NEVER stop. I still feel guilty. I still see you in strangers sometimes. I'll see a woman who reminds me of you and I'll want to talk to her but I know it won't be your voice coming from her. She is not you. No one on earth is you. I could search the entire globe and I still would not find you and that creates a type of loneliness that seems as though it will never fade. My only solace in this is the "hope" Sherri has helped me develop. The hope that I will see you again someday. The hope that someday I will be able to tell you face-to-face and heart-to-heart that I'm so sorry for any moment I made you feel sadness. I have hope that although we couldn't spend all of our years together here on earth, we will eventually be spending eternity together. Beautiful HOPE. Right now, it's all I have. I miss you Momma.

May 05, 2014 8:02 AM

Good morning my friends. I hope that it is in fact a good morning for you. I understand that there may be financial things making this morning not-so-good for some of us. But remember, whatever you're going through, you've gone through it before and you made it through just fine. Focus on that. You will undoubtedly get through it again. Worrying about things that you *know* will eventually be fine such as finances breeds unnecessary frustration and ruins a precious day that didn't have to be ruined. Money problems? We all run into that and although it is easier said than done, just wait, the money will eventually come. It always does. Under eviction? As hopeless as it may seem right now, it will work out. I mean, it *has* to. Car broken down? Just get a ride until you can get your car fixed. You know good and well that you will be back to normal in very little time. The fact of the matter is, if lack of enough money is your *only* problem then you should thank God that you aren't one of the people who awoke this morning in physical pain for whatever reason. Thank God that you didn't wake up this morning just to watch someone you love suffer for whatever reason. Thank God that you didn't wake up lonely because you're in a bad relationship. Thank God that you don't have to spend this day visiting someone you love in a hospital. Thank God that you didn't wake up this morning with problems and worry that money cannot fix. People who woke up this morning facing these things scoff at our petty money problems. So instead of counting the dollars in your pocket today try counting the blessings in your heart. You may find that you have more blessings than money and for that I suggest that you thank God. It can be extremely rough out here on us but if lack of money is the only problem you face today, look up to the Heavens and THANK GOD!

May 05, 2014 9:24 AM

My sister is fighting back and winning. I see the beauty in her aura coming back. Her laugh, her caring attitude, it's all coming back. I thank all of my friends who prayed for my baby sister. God listened and HE is carrying her right now. HE is holding her much too high up for her to be touched by the evil that had engulfed her precious soul. Of course, she is still fighting to be the wonderful person who we all know and love but it is a fact that she is *winning* this fight and she promises to *never* stop fighting. I believe in her. She is one of the strongest people I know and I admire her for that. I can't tell you how wonderful it is to have one of my best friends and biggest supporters on her way back. She is living proof that if you want your life back, JUST GO TAKE IT! I love you Baby Girl!

May 18, 2014 5:59 PM (MF)

What about that "other" side of love? You know when you and your "Boo" have been going at each other's throat verbally for 3 or 4 days. We have been constantly pointing out each other's perceived flaws and just saying unnecessary awful things to each other, telling each other how "sick" of this we are. Lately, I have been so angry with her that I have actually been contemplating my life without her. I have not been finding her as attractive as I usually do because I've been angry with her and I'm even finding her witticisms annoying when I usually find them interesting and charming. She has been saying equally disheartening things to me. Things that I'm almost sure she doesn't mean. But because we are in the middle of an extended argument, I am taking everything she says to heart. We are bringing up the most ridiculous things about each other. We are fighting. I believe we are using each other as "verbal punching bags" because it is time for that. My friends, there is *no way* I'm going to allow this to go *any* further. She is at work right now and after the phone conversation we just had I am sure she is feeling that I may be the most awful person she has ever met. When she gets home I will consciously end this unnecessary battle. I will stop acting as if I couldn't care less if we split up forever. I will stop saying such atrocious things to her and I will ask her forgiveness for my behavior over the past few days. It no longer matters who is right or wrong. My only interest right now is ending this potentially devastating conflict. In complete reality, if I ever lost her I would *never* get over it. I am conscious of the fact that "you don't know what you have until it's gone". Well, I'm going to end this here because I have to get her dinner started and get her house spotless. I'm about to prepare to make her night as pleasant as possible. Perhaps she will resist at first because she is still so angry with me. But I know for a fact that she loves me and within that love she holds a ton of forgiveness. I'm about to go after some of that forgiveness. I'm about to treat her like she deserves to be treated. There is no way I will let such child's play end my relationship. NO WAY!

May 23, 2014 11:10 AM (MF)

"Psst... hey you.... don't give up. Keep swinging!" Easier said than done, right? Most things worth doing are just that. Human battles and mistakes are normal but imploding because of them is *not* normal. One of our greatest gifts from God is the gift of time and the ability to heal and move on. No one's life is perfect, no matter how much some of us attempt to make it seem so. When you're poor, almost every day is a struggle. By "poor" I mean "not rich". I have so very little but with my friends, I share all I have. I truly believe, "As long as one of us got...some of us got" (Tupac) Sometimes I run into situations where I just want to say, "Screw this, I give up!" and then I actually say it. But those are just words. I may step out to regroup but rest assured I'll be back in there fighting the good fight right beside you with everything in me. Perhaps I can barely control my thoughts but I am in complete control of my actions. For some reason, I am naturally drawn to the downtrodden. I feel a deep need to fight for those who do not have the ability, for whatever reason, to fight for themselves. It is not the title of "Hero" that I seek. But I wholeheartedly seek the titles of "Brother", "Dad", "Friend". Everybody likes to feel needed but no one likes to need. I enjoy helping someone who "needs" to borrow money but I absolutely abhor "needing" to borrow it myself. Such is life in "our" world.

What you may be going through is nothing new. That feeling of anger or heartache or even the feeling of being "stuck" and not knowing what your next move in life should be. The key word is "move". Evolve. Stop wallowing in the same old bullshit every day, arguing with the same people and being hurt by the same people. Look at that person who you're arguing with, why are they on your level? It's because you need to raise your level. There comes a time in life when you must ask yourself two important questions..."What the hell am I doing?" and "Why the hell am I doing it?" If you can't answer those two questions with *clear* positive answers then it's time for a change. And no one in the world can change what you're doing but *you*. Stop sitting back and waiting on your life to change. Control the change and *make* it happen. I wonder how many times God has said," Stop asking me for the strength and ability to change when I've already given them to you. You just need to utilize them." The first thing you need to do is *stand up*. The second thing you need to do is *move*. I promise you, you'll be amazed at what you're capable of when you realize just how capable you truly are. Think positively my friends.

May 24, 2014 2:14 PM

Three words. When spoken together they are the most powerful and telling words in language. Sometimes they are thrown around so much that it almost makes them meaningless but when they are spoken together with feeling and commitment it reminds us that they are in fact the most meaningful three words ever. For me, they are reserved for when they are absolutely necessary. I do not use them in just any old situation. In fact, I hate using them and I don't use them very often. They make me feel vulnerable, like I'm opening myself up too much. When they are spoken to me I immediately begin to feel awkward. Not so much because they were said to me but more because I feel obligated to say them back, whether I mean them or not. These are words that you must acknowledge when they are said to you because ignoring them is not what normal people do. To some, saying these words exposes a "softness" that a lot of people don't want anyone to know they have. To others, they use these words as often as they speak. I always tell my wife that she uses these words too much but lately I've been looking at the other side of that spectrum and thinking that perhaps it is me who doesn't use them enough. However, I know for a fact that I *cannot* use them if I don't wholeheartedly mean them. I can honestly say, if I say these words to you, I not only mean them but I absolutely feel toward you what they represent. Myself, I only say these words to people who already know that I feel that way about them although there are some people whom I've *never* said them to, but I could, and honestly mean them.

May 26, 2014 9:01 AM

I don't understand a woman who keeps getting hurt by the same man over and over and over. It would seem that at some point it becomes her own fault. It would also seem that at some point she would reach into her box of "self-worth" and pull out some pride and then use it accordingly. What has you thinking that you are not worth more than that? Love? If you think it's "love" then you have no idea what the difference between "love" and "stupidity" is. I'm sorry but I can't find one kind way to tell a woman that is constantly being hurt by a man to *STOP THE MADDNESS!* Do you think that eventually he will stop all the bullshit and start to treat you right? Really? Perhaps you should look up Albert Einstein's definition of "insanity" because it fits what you're doing perfectly. Is it because you have children with him? That's not a "reason", that's just an "excuse". It's an excuse to fight for something that even your children would tell you to give up on. If you don't think your children see your heartache, then you're wrong. They see it and they don't really understand it. What you *need* to do is wake up one morning and go stand in front of the mirror and wholeheartedly tell yourself, "I am worth so much more than this. I deserve so much more than this. Today, I will take my heart back from him." You need to not only *say* it but you need to *mean* it. Cut him off. Don't go through one more day of heartache that you don't deserve. Do it for your children, do it for your future, but mostly do it for yourself. Quit committing emotional suicide over and over. Quit wasting time trying to provide hope to something that is so totally hopeless. It will, no doubt, be rough at first. But the sorrowful feelings of leaving this dude alone will only happen once, while the sorrowful feelings of him hurting you will happen over and over and over until you care about yourself enough to say, *"THAT'S IT...NO MORE!!!"*, and truly mean it. I swear, you're worth it.

May 30, 2014 5:17 PM

I am not one to question the Almighty's decisions, however, perhaps He made it much too easy to have children. I doubt there would be any such thing as Welfare if you had to work for a living to have children. These broke bitches out here are just popping out children who have no chance in hell of being *anything* but a burden on society. They barely even care about these kids. These kids are undisciplined and just bad as fuck.

These parasites don't want a job and raising a kid is just that, *a job*. That's why they don't raise them. They let them raise themselves. They have children and then immediately start holding their sorry hand out like they're owed something. I have very little patience with these bitches. They're not even trying, and that's what makes it *completely* their own fault. Fucking worthless cockroaches! I totally understand that there are some men who fit this criteria also.

Jun 02, 2014 8:28 AM

There is nothing wrong with me. I'm being quiet simply because I want to be. I am trying to get rid of the part of my personality that makes me say things that I shouldn't say. Soon, I will attempt to *seriously* change my life (again). I plan on becoming much more responsible than I've ever been. There are a few vices in my world that I must get rid of if I am to accomplish the drastic changes that I am seeking. I must stop looking at every confrontation presented to me as "all-out war". I must learn how to control my feelings better. I am an "over-reactor" by nature. Most of the time I take things said to me or about me much too personally and I feel a strong desire to crush whomever is attempting to hurt me. It doesn't matter how small and petty the challenge is, I will, no doubt, overreact to it. I must work on fixing that. I really dislike that about myself. I need to get out of this house more often. I have a routine of going to work, coming home, computer, TV, garage, kitchen, a little more TV, a shower, some more computer, back to the garage, into the kitchen again, down to the basement and *repeat*. I must admit that I am never really bored but I need to change. I don't know what makes me so antisocial. I have the unfortunate ability to totally shut someone out of my life forever for slightest hint of disrespect and I use that sad ability without even thinking sometimes. I will go years without having a relationship with someone whom I think I truly care about just because of something they said to me. It's gotten to the point to where I'm not really sure who I even "truly" care about anymore. Sometimes I ask myself, "Am I just wasting my life?". But I can never answer that. I don't know if I should force myself to do things that I have absolutely no desire to do. I'm not real sure if I'm content or not. I hope I find out before it's too late. I can hear the "clock" ticking. *TICK TOCK TICK TOCK.* But how do you hurry up and do nothing? How do you hurry up and follow the same path that you've been following and at the same speed? Although I am *sure* I could have done more with my life than I have done, perhaps this is it for me. Perhaps, this is supposed to be my life. Perhaps I am right where I'm supposed to be. I wish I knew for sure.

Jun 02, 2014 8:35 PM

It seems as if we are damn near best friends while we are working together but once you quit or get fired we drift apart and become damn near strangers again. Such is life, I guess.

Jun 03, 2014 8:35 AM

Settling "differences" with someone instantly makes you feel better.

Jun 05, 2014 6:33 AM

Yesterday morning, I got ready to go to work with my pants and draws and shirt and socks & shoes, etc. My wife takes me to work and we stop at a gas station. I went into the gas station and made a purchase. I came back out and got into her truck. She drove me to work. While sitting in the parking lot of my job I began to feel something moving inside my pants leg. At first I'm almost sure it's my imagination because it is moving up by my lower thigh. Then I confirm the fact that something is in my pants. I began to violently shake my leg while screaming like a scared bitch. I shake and I shake and suddenly my wife and I see a huge butterfly fly out the bottom of my pants and fly out the window. I am deathly afraid of those damn things and *always* have been. For some reason, my wife found her husband about to pass out to be extremely funny. We cannot figure out how it got there or when it could have possibly gotten there. It makes me feel better to say that it was my mother saying hello to me. Good morning my friends!

Jun 06, 2014 4:53 PM

I hate when I can't find something and I spend about 15 minutes blaming my wife for losing it and when I find it I realize I put it there. It's even worse when she is standing there when I find it and she knows I put it there. I swear she loses *everything* but every great once and a while it will be me who misplaced it. That's why I blame her every time, because I'm right most of the time. When I'm wrong, I do the 'manly" thing, I quickly change the subject.

Jun 11, 2014 7:50 AM

If being filthy rich means that you have to be a greedy, selfish, uncaring, asshole of a person who thinks *every* poor person is just a lazy loser who isn't trying hard enough, then I *still* want to be rich. The devil would never let me be filthy rich. I'd help way too many people. Perhaps even to my own detriment.

Jun 15, 2014 8:26 AM

I miss my father. Just in case people who have passed away can read social media, I want you to know that I miss your infectious laughter that would originate from your soul. There are so many good memories that I am remembering today. Remember when we would battle each other at Spades and Casino for hours? We were both so competitive. Remember how proud of ourselves we would get when we finished putting siding or a roof on someone's house? Remember how you used to tell me that you loved me and that you were proud of me almost every time you seen me? Remember every time I would get paid I would come hunt you down and give you $20 or $30 just because I knew you needed it? The appreciation that I would see in your eyes was mostly the reason that I kept doing that. I needed to see that even more than you needed the money. Remember when you told me that I was the only positive thing in your life? I didn't understand that at the time but I want you to know that I fully understand what you were saying now. I can remember quite a few times when you were there for me when I needed you so badly. I depended on you more than you will ever know. I know how much you wanted to earn my respect and well, you can rest assured that your namesake will never speak of you without respect and love until my own demise. Happy Father's Day Pops. We all miss you every day.

Jun 16, 2014 7:46 AM

I try to never underestimate the intelligence of keeping my opinions to myself and keeping my mouth shut. Although it is sooo hard for me, I'm getting better at it. My favorite question to myself is, "Who are you to judge?" I don't like to carry around a "book bag" full of flaws while judging how someone else chooses to handle their own flaws. I often stand in my mirror at the end of the day and say, "Okay, you've spent the day judging folks and telling people they need to improve their decision making, now, let's talk about what *you're* doing and how *we* could improve."

Jun 22, 2014 8:37 AM

I want you to love me but I don't have the mental capacity to do what it takes to make you love me. I want to be there for you without you asking me to but I don't have the energy required to make that happen. I want you to forgive me but I don't have the ability to honestly ask you to. I know it needs fixed but I don't possess the tools to fix it. I am emotionally selfish. Perhaps selfish to the point of it being a mental condition. I want to care that you rarely even speak to me but I don't know where to get that sort of feeling from because unfortunately I don't think it is within me. Perhaps you share these same feelings towards me. It seems that some people are born to do certain things, like play basketball, be a mechanic, be a doctor, or even be a criminal. Perhaps I was born just to create you. Please know that I will die knowing I should have been a better and more caring father. Know that I fought my selfish tendencies every day and every day I lost. I have no control over this and God knows that I wish I did. Love. I'm not really good at showing it but I know I feel it towards you inside this twisted heart and mind of mine. I just wish things were different but they probably never will be. And I'm so sorry for that. I know that I care because if I didn't, I would not be seeking your forgiveness. I will never give up on trying to rectify this situation but if I fall short before my demise I just ask that you try to have more understanding than hatred for me. And know that I accept all responsibility for how you felt about me.

Jul 04, 2014 6:26 PM

People always ask me this question, "Why do you always look so mean?" It is amazing how much I'm asked that question. Sometimes I'll say "What's up?" to someone and they will automatically think it was a hostile "What's up?". Sometimes I have to go out of my way and start smiling like a dumb ass at somebody just because I don't want them to think that. Then they look at me like I'm weird or something. I, like anyone else, can be hostile. However, I spend 99% of my life *not* being hostile. I love interesting conversation, no matter who it's with. I listen closely when I'm being spoken to. I, like everyone else, like to be complimented although to most I pretend it means nothing to me. I like to give out deserving compliments because I know it's an easy way to make someone's day perhaps. And I love doing that. I notice people giving it there all when others might not notice and I let them know that for all it's worth, I notice you. My point is, in spite of my unintentional mean mug, I could wholeheartedly get along with any good person on earth.

Jul 06, 2014 7:58 AM

The Lord is here this Sunday morning. No matter your degree of belief in religion, sometimes, even *you* feel His presence. Sometimes He makes His blessings so undeniable that you just have to look up and raise your hands and say, "I feel You Lord! I know that You're in me today and at this moment!" For any suffering that I go through, I love when You let me know that no amount of suffering can prevent the euphoric feeling I get when You tap me on my shoulder and whisper into my ear, "Relax, I've got this." The feeling of believing and knowing that those words are true. So true. Although I backslide, although I rarely speak of You, although I sometimes run and hide from You, today, I am not ashamed to say that in spite of my sinful ways, I don't even have to ask You for help, it's just there. It's always been there. And when this kind of help is there, it's obvious where it is coming from. This kind of help cannot be described with words like "luck" or "chance" or "coincidence". This help is undeniably divine. On this Sunday morning I am putting aside *all* doubt and replenishing the good in my soul with thoughts of our Lord and with thoughts of how divinely blessed I truly am. Yes, you can best believe, *THE LORD IS HERE THIS SUNDAY MORNING*. I might go to church today. God bless my friends.

Jul 11, 2014 4:39 PM

LeBron left us for someone else. He went and had a couple of children (championships), realized he liked us more and so he's coming back to us. Yeah, when he left us we were angry and thought he was just being a slut but he was so good to us while we were together we will forgive. When he has some children with us, they will mean much more than the children he has with those other people. We are Cleveland fans. We rarely come out on the good side of *anything* and we are willing to do almost anything to win. Even turn a ho into a housewife. *GO BROWNS-CAVS-INDIANS!!!!*

Jul 15, 2014 8:52 AM (MF)

A Noose for Me

I was about 6 years old at the time. My mother and father had recently been divorced and I was staying with a lot of different babysitters while my mom took advantage of her new single life. I don't remember every single babysitter I had but there was one in particular whom I remember vividly. He was one of my mother's friend's relatives. He was white and maybe in his 20's at the time. I have no idea why he was chosen to babysit me. One day in particular is very memorable to me because sometimes we have things happen in our lives that just stick in our memory banks for whatever reason. This day my mother left me with this young man and I guess he decided that on this day he would teach me some sort of evil lesson for some reason. He was babysitting me with one of his friends on this day and he owned what is called an El Camino. It's a car with a bed like a pick-up truck. He and his friend thought it would be fun to put me into the back of his car and drive. I had no security, no seatbelt, not anything to hold on to. Perhaps because I was 6 years old I thought I was about to have some fun. This young man began to drive this car like he was attempting to throw me out of it. He was doing donuts and driving very fast and then slamming on the brake as if he and his friend were getting a thrill out of watching me be more afraid than I had ever been up to that point. I could hear them laughing and calling me a nigger as I screamed and held onto anything I touched for dear life. After they had their fun they took me back to the house they were watching me at and they weren't finished with me. I can remember them continually calling me a nigger and smacking and punching me. One of them came up with the brilliant idea to take me into the basement. They roughly lead me down into the basement and as I cried from sheer terror I saw one of them grab a rope and begin to tie it to a water pipe in that basement. I didn't know it at the time but this man was creating a noose. *A noose for me*. One of them lifted me up and the other one placed the noose around my neck and tightened it and then the other one let me go. And there I hung. I can remember the pain and terror I was feeling as if it were yesterday. I remember them calling me a nigger over and over and I remember them spitting on me as I hung there. As I hung there undoubtedly paralyzed with fear God must have said, "That's enough of this." I could see headlights pull up through the basement window and they saw them too. It was my mother coming to pick me up. One of them hurriedly cut me down and in doing so I fell to the ground and got a gash in my back from something I fell into when I hit the ground. I still carry the slight scar from that gash to this day. I have no idea what they could have told my mother to make her accept the emotional state of her 6-

year-old son. I have no idea how they explained the cut on my back or the ligature marks around my neck but I was never asked what had happened so I assume their lies were sufficient for my mother. After this ordeal I was afraid of any and all 'babysitters". My mother left me with racist psychopaths who did all but kill me, who else would she leave me with? I needed protection and the only person I looked to for that protection was my mother. Unfortunately for me, it was rarely there. It is memories like these that fill me with the knowledge that God has always been there for me. No matter what anyone was doing to me or what I was doing to myself, my God would only let it go so far until he would step in and give me that protection that no one in my life felt I needed. God felt it. And He still feels it. I survived ordeals such as this because I'm supposed to be here. I have work to do in this life. Anytime I make someone feel better than they did just by talking to me, that makes it worth it. Anytime I can share what little I have with someone who feels desperate, that makes it worth it. For whatever reason, God felt that I was worth saving and I will spend the rest of my life recognizing that worth in those around me. God bless you my friends.

Jul 15, 2014 8:37 PM

I don't have to see or talk to you every day to love you.

Jul 17, 2014 6:34 PM

You ever get so fuckin drunk that you stop giving a shit about *anything*? Why is it when you get drunk as hell you always forget about tomorrow? It's like it shuts down every part of your brain that has to do with the future. You wake up like, "Oh shit". "I beat my dad up last night." "And I tried to get with my girl's friend and she tells *everything!*" "And I feel like shit cuz I'm hung over." "There ain't even no pop in this bitch." "Hell naw I don't want a cigarette."

Jul 18, 2014 5:43 PM

Everyone has a story or two that they could share. I just choose to share some of mine with you. Some of my stories will make you cry, some will make you laugh, but they will all give you a glimpse of the world through my own personal perception because they're all true. Every word is from experience and memory. Some of you write unbelievable compliments on some of my posts and like I said, some of them are truly unbelievable to me. To think that somebody like me could ever touch someone in a positive way with just the written word is something that I never imagined I could do. I am writing daily, trying so hard to do something that, in my world, is unheard of. Actually putting action and effort behind a positive idea. I will complete this book. I will do it because it is a part of practicing what I preach. I will do it because I can. Some of you even private message me and show me just mind blowing support. All I can do on your comments is hit the "Like" button but with some of you there is a lot behind hitting that "button". I am overwhelmed with amazement at what I read. My whole point in writing this is to tell you that I truly appreciate your comments and support. I wouldn't even know anyone would be interested in anything I write if not for your interest in some of the hundreds of stories in my head. I thank you my friends. You have no idea what it means to me.

Jul 19, 2014 5:49 PM

You've got to have passion about doing what you do for a living when you aren't getting rich doing it. Even if that passion is forced. Without that passion, you'll give up.

Jul 25, 2014 8:54 PM

I'm glad the police are out so deep tonight. I wish they were like that every damn night. I have people I love out here among these folks acting like animals. I hope they pull *everybody* over, even me. I have a valid driver's license and insurance and I don't carry an illegal gun and I don't murder people so it's not the police I worry about, it's the people they're after who concern me. Come on man, life is too short to behave that way *every* damn day. I pray "the innocent" stay safe.

Jul 30, 2014 6:27 PM (MF)

More than how we were raised, more than where we were raised, more than who our parents are, more than what we look like, much much more than all of that, you and me, we are products of our very own choices. That seems so simple at any age and yet some of our youth, some of them can't grasp it. Young people listen, you'll be considered a "youth" for a very short period of time. You can choose not to let your youth destroy your whole life. And those dudes you run with, those dudes you will die or go to jail for, and of course they would die or go to jail for you, those are just dudes racing you down an unnecessary, life threatening path. In 10 or 15 years, you may not even know where some of those dudes live. You remain friends but you become men. You learn to prioritize. And that just goes for those who make it. You all will have a family to take care of. It will inevitably be your turn to pray every night that your child makes the right choices. A job will inevitably become one of the most important things in your life. How early you realize that will dictate what kind of job you have. You should choose to get prepared for that. It is how you will live *most* of your life. Young people, these are *facts*!

Jul 31, 2014 6:12 PM (MF)

I know it's hard. Believe me when I tell you, I *know* it is *so* hard. Your "boys" are your "boys". How can that *ever* end? You love drinking all the time, being high *all* the time, you love "checkin a nigga" about something. You need "nice" things and minimum wage and the constant grind of a "bullshit" job, it just ain't gonna get it done. Hell, you can make in a day what those "square" dudes make on a paycheck. You feel like, "Fuck jail. It's probably where I belong anyway." You don't care what none of the people who *really* love you say. It's your "Niggas" that matter, your Homeboys. They're the only ones who understand you. You can't change that. Can you? You're living your life like you're banking on not seeing 30 years old. And 40 years old is so far off that you couldn't care less about it. Underestimating the fact that you *will* see both off those ages will be your biggest regret (bar none) when you are sitting there 35 years old, with children that you can't take care of and no education except the half assed effort you gave Stark State. What are you gonna do? You can't live off that woman forever. You certainly can't sell dope forever. The longer you do that, the more it becomes statistically unhealthy in every way. So what are you gonna do? I'll tell you what you're gonna do, you're gonna struggle. Just like me and most of my peers who did what you're doing. Very few of us made it out totally unscathed. We're all doing as best we can these days. Very few of us are doing "what we want". We blew it. And for most of us, it's our biggest regret. That's why I can sit here and tell you that you don't have to blow it. It's not too late for you. You can start by doing this: Go to your mother or your grandmother or sometimes even your "girl", that person in your life that you go to when you need to feel safe and content, that person you take for granted, spend time with them. More time than you ever even thought was possible. Remember how much you hate to see them cry. Because the road you're going down right now, during your journey, it's gonna make them cry a lot. It's gonna hurt them so bad. How can you spend even one moment of your life not caring about that? You can't ignore that. You are *not* having fun. You are ruining your life and hurting the people who *really* love you. That is *all* you're doing. It ain't worth it. It can *never* be worth it. Look up the word "discipline", truly learn it's meaning, and then show some. The clock is ticking my friend. Do it before it's too late.

Aug 04, 2014 9:16 AM

I often get on here and attempt to throw out words of inspiration but every once and a while I have to talk about things that are not so inspirational. What I'm about to write may piss some people off but it is how *most* people feel and most people don't feel it is politically correct to talk about it. But me, I don't give a damn if it's right to talk about it or not. What I *do* give a damn about is the fact that it's the truth...

Why do we as a society cater to these girls who simply choose to be lazy and irresponsible? They don't do shit all week but bum shit off of other people and sit around their depressing house wondering where the next "handout" will come from. On the weekend *nothing* becomes more important than finding a penis to play with. They're not thinking about how they're going to come up with that whopping $20 they pay in rent every month. When they get evicted from public housing they start to get evicted from places all over town because believe it or not, landlords don't like to take care of people by providing them a rent free house for them and their children to tear up. For some reason, landlords really frown upon stuff like that. No car, no food, no school clothes, no sense, no motivation, no shame, but they will have one or two pit bulls and some "dude" living with them. I will *never* understand that. They should be ostracized and treated like pariahs but they are often felt sorry for and given free shit by people who enable their ridiculously counterproductive self-destructive behavior. They have hundreds of excuses as to why they won't get a job and none of them are the *one* that is true, "I'm just too lazy to get it together and every time I hold my hand out people seem to put things in it." The only people in that situation whom I have *any* sympathy for are their children. Most of them have no idea what's going on. In what universe is it a good idea to already have a kid that you can't take care of and then go have two or three more? How is that not a crime? It is in fact a crime for an "absent" father not to get a job and financially take care of his children but it is alright for a "present" mother to be as bummy as she wants to be throughout a kid's whole childhood. They should be made to work a full time job for *any* "benefits" they get and if they don't work the job then they should *GO TO JAIL*. Period. Even if someone else has to find the job for them. They are ridiculous, pathetic and WRONG!

Aug 05, 2014 6:45 PM

Imagine if you will, you're a young lady, you meet a guy whom you like and for whatever reason you decide to have sex with him. As so often happens, you become pregnant. For whatever reason the father leaves. You have the baby with mostly only your family by your side.

After a couple of days, you leave the hospital and go home. You're broke, you're on your own, and you have a newborn baby. I have worked with countless women who were in a similar scenario as this. I see how hard they work. They confide in me about the personal sacrifices they make just to be as happy as they can every day. These women are modern day warriors. The stories they tell me are nothing short of inspiring. Inspiring because in spite of it all, they are in here every day with a ton of invisible weight on their shoulders. I know that weight is there partly because they told me it was. Still though, for at least eight hours almost every day they are in there with a smile on their faces and ready to go to work. Ready to provide even if no one else will. Although they may need help from time to time, they are giving it their all, and it is all but easy. It is not easy to do what they do almost *every* day. I see these ladies. I know their story. I've seen them set their angst aside and perform their job to the best of their ability. I've been listening to and watching these ladies for almost seven years now. I never knew that there were so many of them. They have taught me that you don't have to just sit there and be a "victim". You can do something about it. You can do *all* you can for your children. I hear all kinds of stories from these ladies but by far, the tons of stories I've heard involve their children and the sacrifices they make for them. Most of which, their children don't even know their making.

These women have shown me something that I didn't see a whole lot growing up and that is a mother fighting back and realizing that her children are worth all she goes through each and every day. Never forgetting or giving up on that. Never stopping for lack of anything. Be it a man or money problems or a sick relative or sometimes even being sick themselves. These women do every day what I'm almost sure that I myself could not do. When I go home after work, I relax. I couldn't imagine not being able to do that. I know the difference between these ladies and the ones I wrote about in my previous post. These ladies often thank me after we talk with each other. But little do they know, it is me who should thank them for teaching me and opening my eyes one incredible story at a time.

Aug 08, 2014 10:13 AM

These troubles are not here to stay

They are just passing through

As they often do

I've seen them before and I'll see them again

I see better days coming as I look within

I remain hopeful...always hopeful

Aug 08, 2014 5:07 PM

It doesn't matter how heartless you try to be or how hard and tough you think you are; *LOVE* will bring the biggest beast to their knees. It will make you say things and act in ways that will cause you to question your own personality.

Aug 09, 2014 5:39 PM

Sometimes I just don't feel like talking on the phone or texting. That's all. I swear, it's nothing personal. When I feel like this, I wouldn't be good conversation anyway. When I call someone, I don't take their voicemail answering their phone too personal. I realize, they just might feel the way I do sometimes.

Aug 12, 2014 7:16 AM

I wrote this about 20 years ago. Well before everyone had cell phones. I have a sibling who is going through some emotionally trying times right now and she specifically requested that I do this. She has always liked this poem. She even had it framed and hanging on her wall many many years ago. Personally, I don't like writing rhyming poetry because the rhyming of words restricts what you can write. And I'm not very good at that. We love you Rosetta Mae Cooper.

Hopeless

I have an uncontrollable urge to cry

I don't know what to do

But I know what I want to do...die

I don't want to sleep because my dreams tell me lies

I wake up and the truth fills my heart through my eyes

Oh the things I would do differently if I had her back again

I would love her, yet not too much, kind of like a loyal friend

I can't believe anyone else in the world feels the way that I do

I can't believe, all of this pain...she doesn't feel a little of it too

Everything reminds me of her...everything I see

That chair, that picture, even my own hands and everything on TV

Every time the phone rings..."Please God, let it be her"

Even if she just breathes to me and doesn't say a word

She is a drug that I am hopelessly addicted to

She doesn't say anything yet she controls my every move

I only want to talk to people whom I know that she knows

I find myself only going places that I know that she goes

Another relationship? Not for a very long time

That's if I live through this because suicide is consuming my mind

I listen for the telephone as I look out the door and cry

I can't go anywhere just in case she decides to come by

When I see her, then what...will she listen to my pleas

As I cry "Baby, I'm sorry"...looking up at her from my knees

Being alone is torture...for my thoughts won't let me rest

No matter what I think about it ends with my own death

I think I love her family when I couldn't tolerate them before

I find myself loving everyone just a little bit more

Maybe she would have sympathy if I could make her see...

The torment I am going through is slowly killing me

I know I am insane as I sit and cry in the dark

But something says, "No you're not. You just have a broken heart."

Be strong...very strong...for I am living proof

That a broken heart is like any break...eventually it heals too

Remember "THIS TOO SHALL PASS" and keep this thought in focus

In time, I swear, you won't believe how things seemed so hopeless

Aug 15, 2014 12:24 PM

I personally believe way too much emphasis is put on the contributions of a "boss". Why are they undeservingly treated as if they are some sort of god? It's a trip the way they go around thinking everyone who "works" for them cares when they talk about their home life, family and what they like to do. *Everyone* has a home life, family and things they like to do. I care much more about the people right beside me in the trenches doing all we can to make that "boss" seem like they're doing a good job, whether they are doing a good job or not. Don't get me wrong, I believe a "boss" deserves a lot of respect and attention but that person busting their ass and making a quarter of the money the "boss" makes deserves just as much attention and respect. Without those who are being lead, a leader is useless.

Aug 17, 2014 8:37 AM

I'm going to church for the first time in over 25 years. Clyde Jr. and church, this ought to be an interesting combination. I will be sure to let God know that I am at church today to learn how to be a soldier against evil. I am here for my orders. Whatever they may be. I am here because I *need* to be. God bless you my friends. I will be praying for *all* of us.

Aug 20, 2014 5:23 PM

You got it so good. You just need to recognize it. There are folks out here who would absolutely love to trade problems with you. Recognize it!

Aug 21, 2014 9:57 PM

Random fact: I sleep with a pillow between my knees because I don't like for my knees to touch for some reason

Sep 01, 2014 11:56 AM

Hello my friends. Although my book isn't finished yet I just wanted to talk to you for a minute. I'm afraid that what I always thought would be impossible is becoming reality. My relationship with Sherri is all but over. Although there is plenty of blame to go around, I won't waste your time with the details of our relationship's demise. I met Sherri in 1993. We were friends, then boyfriend and girlfriend, and then husband and wife. We have been through a lot together both good and bad. She was my best friend for a very long time. We started having major problems in our relationship not long ago. I have chosen to end it. I have never really been single before. I've never lived on my own. To be honest with you, I'm cautiously looking forward to it. I realize that the end of such a long relationship will bring on feelings of heartache, loneliness, and depression. These are things that I do not look forward to but they are tunnels that I *must* go through to get to where I need to be. I must keep in focus the fact that I will be happy again. I will cry and wonder if I made the right decision but ultimately, I will be happy again. I have been through a lot in my life and I've come out of it stronger each and every time. I have absolutely no doubt that this is what I will do again. I have very little animosity towards Sherri. I do not blame her for any trouble that I have ever faced. I do not wish that any harm come to her. I know it is not up to me to punish *anyone* regardless of their behavior. It just isn't working out and therefore it is best that we go our separate ways. That's all there is to it. I have a lot, and I mean *a lot* of work to do to continue becoming a better person. This is what I plan on spending the majority of my "free" time on. I will admit, I have built my life around the premise of "being there" for anyone who ever needed me and I am now realizing that I have to come up with some way to "be there" for myself. I have way too much pride to ask for a shoulder to cry on. I am way too stubborn to admit that I am falling apart inside. I always claim to "enjoy" loneliness and now fate has put me in a position where it is "put up or shut up" time. It is time for me to face a new level of loneliness, a level I've never really faced before. For the next few months my life will be awkward and disoriented in ways I've never seen it be. I will face feelings that I've never really faced before. I know that I have so many good people in my life and I know I can talk to any one of you about what I'm going through but if you know me at all then you know I will not burden the already burdened with my personal problems. I am on social media telling you my story because I know that it will make others see that the end of a relationship does not have to mean the end of a life. And perhaps some of your words will help this notion sink into my own heart, reassuring me that life is *always* worth all the effort you can muster. We all talk to each other about our problems and right now, this one is mine. I am at the beginning of a road that I simply *must* go down. I am not sure how long this road is going to be but I do know for sure that most of it will be rough and most of it will make me want to just give up on myself. Although I don't like to admit it, maybe I am in fact looking for a little sympathy and words of encouragement. Perhaps this is my way of reaching out into the darkness and trying to pull back a little closure and understanding. Perhaps I will regret putting this on here one day. But at the present time, this feels right. Who knows what the future holds? I will be judged by some of you and I am okay with that. Some of you will sit there and read this and wonder how I can put something so personal about my marriage on here. I've never claimed to be perfect and if you've read any of my previous posts you know I am far from perfect, leaning much more towards a complete screw up. I am a work in progress. I am a strong man with unlimited potential. This is *my* life and it's the only one I get. I cannot let misery just take over my one chance at life and just control it. I will not. I will take it one day at a time. I will get back up and dust myself off while still reaching down to pull as many people as I can onto their feet. This is how I am built. These things are what I want to have on my resume` when I reach the Pearly Gates. I know that God will know that although the first part of my life had me lying down in unspeakable sin, eventually I did all I could to stand up and atone with every breath I had left. Thank you for allowing me to lean on you my friends. God bless us all.

Sep 01, 2014 3:59 PM

You just never know what the future holds

For the future has not been told

Sometimes you're where you thought you'd never be

Seeing things you thought you'd never see

Feeling ways that seem so strange

Dealing with life and its love of change

The way things were may not be like they are

And if the change hurts...it's bound to leave a scar

But scars fade...leaving only a faint reminder...

Of how cruel life can be before it inevitably gets kinder

Love is EVERYWHERE. Thank you my friends.

Sep 01, 2014 6:31 PM

The Lord is at work my friends. I've got a feeling He has a miracle in store. Once again holding me up.

Sep 03, 2014 8:49 AM

Hello friends. First of all, let me say that I promise never to put a post up like the one I put the other day again. I regret putting it on here just like I thought I would. Sherri and I have been dealing with a certain "problem" for a lot of years. I won't say what the "problem" is but I will say that it has brought us to the edge of ending our relationship before and this time we went over the edge. The other night I decided to sit down with Sherri and all other people involved and have a heart to heart like we've never had before. We agreed, we disagreed, we cried, we laughed but we gave resolving this "issue" more effort than we've ever given it. We found out some things about each other and ourselves that we didn't even know. We worked on it for our marriage's sake. Me and Sherri are fine now. I believe the almost 20 year "problem" we had, finally ended the other night with a tearful group hug. Having said all that, I just want you to know that I used to think, "I talk to and help so many people but who is here to "help" me." Well, over the past couple of days, I found out. I was overwhelmed by the show of support on that post and in private messages. I couldn't believe that so many of you were willing to give me however much time out of your own life I may have needed. It totally reassured me that any sacrifice I make for anyone is worth it. I feel renewed and stronger than ever before. The other night, Sherri and I made God our marriage counselor and in just a couple of hours he helped us wash away a problem that we'd been having forever. *Only* God could have done that. We are meant to be together and together we shall remain. Once again, I'm sorry and thank you so much for caring.

Sep 17, 2014 8:41 AM (MF)

Change is so difficult. Perhaps that's why so many of us fail and give up on making changes. Whether it be deciding to quit smoking or cursing or deciding to eat right and begin exercising regularly. It could be changing the way we handle certain situations such as how we treat people, going out of our way to acknowledge people whom everyone else is ignoring or controlling your anger and your words. It is so hard to "confront" someone who has a bad attitude with your own good attitude. That doesn't always work. Some people are simply incorrigible. I often literally tell myself, " You will *not* be in this bad mood." Not only do I say it but I act upon it. I've learned how to stand up to bad "anything" with good "something". I *do not* argue with strangers. I ignore folks who cut me off in traffic or pull out in front of me and start going even less than the speed limit. I am getting so good at totally controlling my mood. I still have work to do but like with any major change, it won't happen overnight. I am realizing that money does not control my life. I don't need it to be happy. *Nothing* materialistic controls my happiness. I work as hard as I can and make as much money as I can and then I sit back and let the chips fall where they may. They usually fall where they are supposed to. When they don't, I adjust. I stay positive about everything and I let God control anything that attempts to bring me down. I am *all* about laughter and smiling. It's what I bring when I come. Good luck staying in a bad mood if I'm around. I see a bad mood from someone and I attack it with overwhelming positivity. The other morning, I was standing in line at McDonald's and I was about the fourth person in a line of about six. You could tell that people were beginning to become impatient with how long it was taking for us to be served. An elderly gentleman walked up to the counter in front of everyone and asked for a coffee and the worker quickly obliged him. There was one guy a couple of people ahead of me in the line who began to flip out about it. He started cussing and saying how wrong it was for this old man to just jump in front of everyone and get served. He was a black guy maybe in his late 40's. He was the only one saying anything about it and then he started to turn around complaining and looking for someone who maybe wanted to complain with him. He looked right at me and said, " This shit ain't right. He should have to wait like everybody else." Perhaps he was right but I looked at him and said, " It's alright Brother. If this is the worst thing that happens to us today, we should end the day feeling blessed." A few folks in the line looked at me and smiled while the angry gentleman, realizing he had absolutely no support with his anger, turned away from me and stood there for about ten more seconds and then angrily left the restaurant. After he left, one lady said, " I'm glad he left" and everyone else began to agree with her and talk about what I said to him. When I got up to the counter to order my food the worker thanked me. That is part of my "changing". A few years ago I would have been cussing everybody out even louder than the guy who was obviously upset when he entered the restaurant. Being positive doesn't cost anything and it is a wonderful feeling. Growing positivity from a negative foundation is not always easy to do but it is certainly worth any and all effort you can give it. Never mistake a bad mood for a bad life. "Life" lasts until you die while "moods" last sometimes mere moments. Life is a gift from God and the ability to change and adjust ourselves to stay happy no matter what is part of that gift. Some people equate money with happiness but if this is true then how can I have so much happiness with so little money? It's because I search for positivity and I usually find it even if I have to create it from the most negative of situations. It's just one of the positive changes I'm making within my life. Positivity is contagious and I want *everyone* to catch it from me.

Sep 19, 2014 10:45 AM

Everything always works out whether I worry about it or not. And since worrying is annoying...I smile.

Sep 24, 2014 9:19 AM

Two young men lost their lives the other night attempting to rob a gas station. These boys weren't "monsters". I could have easily been one of them 20 years ago. Was I a "monster"? No, no I was not. I was lost in a world that does not even recognize the definition of the word "consequences". I was doing what everyone else around me was doing. Was I a criminal? Yes, I was. Whether I deserved to die for my criminal behavior or not is based solely on your own opinion. As I sit back now and ponder the life that me and my "friends" were leading I realize that I am simply lucky. I refuse to just judge these two young men and call them "animals" and leave it at that. They were our children. They were an example of the countless children who are on these streets and desperate for help and desperate for someone to provide them with a reason to make better choices. These kids feel hopeless, and folks who feel hopeless care very little about consequences. I am not making excuses for these young men's actions that so tragically cost them their lives, but I feel compelled to ask, "What brought them to that?" What made robbing that gas station worth it to them? Perhaps it was their lack of understanding that the consequences could be so severe. Perhaps they felt that they had no reason to even care about the consequences. Some of us act like there is no way that could have been "our" children. When I first heard about it, I immediately prayed to God that none of my own children were involved. For a moment, I was worried. Some people say, "These boys got what they deserved." Those who make statements like that should be careful. There are a lot of us who hope that we never really get what we truly "deserve". A lot of us weren't *always* as mature and clear thinking as we are now. How many of us are guilty of turning an innocent person into a victim? I know I am. Looking back on my life, I pray that I *never* get what I truly deserve. Fortunately for me, I have made it to a point in my life where I request "forgiveness" for my past actions more than "mercy" for what I do now. These boys are not heroes by any stretch of the imagination. But perhaps they too were victims. These boys were lost. And why were they "lost"? That is the root question. What makes our community so hopeless that our children are running around welcoming tragedy? Welcoming prison. Welcoming death. Is it lack of good role models? Is it lack of any real opportunity? "Why should I care about living life when life isn't worth living?" Every question has an answer. They *need* an answer to that one. Again, I am *not* making excuses for these boys' actions and I totally realize that their victim did exactly what he *had* to do but it is still so very sad and tragic *all the way around* and any human being can see that. Whether you show mercy and have respect for these boys' families or not, as a human being, you can at least feel some of their pain. Unfortunately, it seems that all we as a community can do is sit back and wait for it to happen again and again. These young men could easily have been one of my children or their victim could easily have been me. I can't ignore that. And frankly, it scares the hell out of me.

Sep 28, 2014 7:58 AM

My options are only limited by my own personal motivation. My success is dictated by the amount of work I am willing to put in. I cannot let someone else's doubt cause me to doubt myself. Those who say "You can't do it" are ignorant. They're ignorant because they equate my drive to theirs. I must become proof. Proof that I am bigger than this. I will never stop anything because of the thought, "What will people think?" I will begin every endeavor with "This is me, take it or leave it" I will not censor myself and water down my thoughts with "You can't say that." I will work, work, work. Work on my attitude and work on getting better at every single thing I do. I will never stop improving because those who stop improving have either given up or become perfect. Perfection is not possible and giving up is not optional. Every day I will have my eyes and mind wide open to improve myself this day, this hour and this moment. Although I hate using the term "Haters" I know there will be some. There are folks whose only mission in life seems to be to do that. There are those who will tell me, "You are wasting your time." and I will believe them, until my conversation with them stops. Time spent trying to become a better and more productive person is never wasted. I will not succeed at everything I try but only I can choose to give up. No one can succeed for me and no one can give up for me. I will not *ever* blame others for my own personal choices. My thoughts and choices are mine. I own them. Be they good or bad. I am me. I have options and I am in complete control of Clyde McCrae Jr.

Oct 12, 2014 8:48 AM

There isn't anything too much worse than someone in "authority" trying to tell me how to be a leader. It creates a mixture of anger, humor, and confusion all at once. It also tells me that this person knows *nothing* about me.

Oct 14, 2014 9:54 AM

We go through some sort of "hell" that seems like it will never end. We go to sleep at night with hope that a new day will bring about cures to all that ails us. We wait days and sometimes even weeks or months for our circumstances to change. Sometimes life pours salt into wounds by piling more on top of an already mind-numbing load. We start feeling like, any minute, we're going to "break". It gets to a point where the smallest of annoyances has the potential to set us off and cause us to temporarily lose control. It has piled up and now we must "dump". Dump about anyone or anything and everything. We're fed up. We're stressed out. Our emotional trunk is full yet filling more. We're wondering if things will ever be "normal" again. Of course, we know that we've been extremely stressed before and we made it through without hurting anyone but *this* time is different. This time it feels like we are on the verge of losing it more than ever. But we're not. We've been here before and we constantly realize that. Realizing that helps us maintain control. We know that tomorrow is a new day, with a new plan and a fresh start if we want it. We know that yesterday's troubles may still linger but every day they are being replaced by today's hope. We all know this. We all believe this. It's what keeps us going. It's our "reason". God gave us other human beings to love and to love us and that gives us purpose. We know that. We fight through troubles with all we have because it is our purpose. It is what we do. We face troubles with hope and purpose behind us. We expect to prevail, and because this is our expectation, we always do. And we always will.

Oct 17, 2014 6:30 PM

You always say, "I don't care what *anybody* thinks about me."

I'll bet you do. You won't admit it, but I'll bet you do.

Oct 17, 2014 6:41 PM

I can remember when "Friday night" meant something to me.

Oct 25, 2014 12:25 PM

The most generous people in the world are the ones who have basically nothing. Their appearance may be ragged but their soul is so very pristine.

Oct 26, 2014 8:41 AM (MF)

I was 19 years old and my friend Dave was about the same age as me when he voluntarily took a fall for me. I had met Dave about 3 years before that when he started dating my younger sister. We would eventually form a close friendship that has lasted all the way up to this very minute and counting. Dave and I were good friends as well as "partners in crime". Most of the ignorant crimes I committed when I was younger, I was with Dave. Dave, in fact, introduced me to my wife Sherri. Dave and I would be all over this city robbing, stealing, assaulting, destroying property, selling drugs and just being all around scum. One day we were at Dave's father's house just looking for something to "get into" and his father had a rifle in his house and I decided that we were going to take that rifle that night and "end it all". We were going to walk around a neighborhood with that loaded rifle and literally shoot the very first person we came into contact with. It would not matter who it was. As soon as we saw them, we were to kill them. The neighborhood is where Walmart now sits on Rt 62. I believe it was Hills at the time. We walked up and down a lot of streets and we saw absolutely no one. Not one soul. It was 3 or 4 o'clock in the morning so there wouldn't be many people out anyway. We eventually came upon Hills' parking lot and we saw one car in the whole parking lot. We thought that the person driving the car was working inside Hills so we decided to wait for them inside their car and when they would come out, it would happen. We waited inside that car for about an hour or 2 and we decided to go somewhere else. As we walked I carried this huge rifle and Dave walked beside me. When we reached the back of Hills I noticed a car riding down Harmont slowly. I then saw that it was a police car. Like the coward I was, I quickly handed the gun to Dave and for some reason he took it. The police car turned down the street we were on and the officers saw me and Dave. They lit us up with their lights and got out of their car and told us to stop. Dave had shoved that rifle down the front of his pants and it was noticeable all the way down his pant leg. We were about 15 yards from the officers when one them asked Dave, "What do you have in your pants?" Dave calmly replied, "A gun." Dave pulled the gun out to show the officers and both of them immediately pulled their guns out and started yelling for him to "DROP IT!" Dave slowly set the gun on the ground and the officers told us both to get on the ground. While we were down on the ground I started to tell Dave that we should just run. I told him that as soon as I say, we were to just run. Dave agreed and so I waited for what I thought would be a good opportunity to get away. The officers came over to us and stood us up. I don't know why they wouldn't just put handcuffs on us immediately, but they didn't. One officer had me by the arm while the other one put Dave up against their car and began to frisk him. In my ignorant mind this was the "opportunity". I broke loose from the officer who had me and then I pushed the officer who had Dave so Dave could get away from him and then I ran for about 10 or 20 yards before I noticed Dave didn't run. He chose not to run. He would later tell me that his legs "just wouldn't move". Once I realized Dave wasn't running I decided to stop running myself. The officer who was holding me grabbed me and began to show me why that whole night was a bad idea. He handcuffed me and all I will say is that he didn't like me and he physically showed me that. After his partner secured Dave and put him in the back of the car, he came over and began to physically show me that *he* wasn't too fond of me either. They threw me into the back of the car practically on top of Dave. There we were, two dangerous idiots, and me beaten up, piled into the back of a police car on our way to jail. Dave was charged with Carrying a Concealed Weapon and I was charged with Obstruction, Resisting Arrest and a few other things. Dave's charge, which should have been mine, was a felony that would send him to prison for 9 months. Although this happened some 24 years ago I still cringe when I think about what Dave and I was about to do. I'm so thankful that God put *no one* in our evil, violent path that night. I sit here today and I can't believe that that was me. If God weren't so merciful I along with Dave would probably be on Death Row right now. Obviously, that's not what God had in store for me. My brother had just gone to prison for murder 5 years before this incident and I was sure my fate would eventually be similar. In fact, I was going to see to it. I was so young and lost. Going to jail for this taught me nothing. For years after this incident I would be doing all I could to prove that I was unhappy and it was everybody else's fault but mine. Anyone who knows me knows that I am far from that person I was back then. I am a new Clyde McCrae Jr. A compassionate, caring person who would never purposely hurt anyone. To this day, I don't understand why I did some of the things I did. Perhaps this is why I can understand that young adults do things that ruin their lives and the lives of others, but I will never know "why". I don't even know why or even how I was like I was. When I think about the younger me I don't know why he was acting the way he was. But I do know what he was lacking, and that was love. He never saw it, so he never showed it. I would eventually figure out on my own that I am surrounded by love. Eventually, with God's grace, I would realize that life is precious. *All life.* I learned that on my own. I'm just glad I didn't learn it while sitting on Death Row.

Oct 29, 2014 10:55 AM (MF)

It was 1993. I had just met Sherri literally a couple of months before. I always carried a .38 Snub Nose Revolver on me because, well, because I was a moron. I continually put myself in predicaments that made me feel as if I needed this sort of protection on me. I would always say,

"I would rather get caught with it than without it." Sherri and I had no place of our own to stay so we would often stay with one of my relatives in Highland Park. This particular relative was on crack so I knew we could stay there and have the freedom to do the ignorant things we did with impunity. One night, Sherri and I was in my relatives' bedroom and I was messing around with my gun. My father was in the living room with some woman who I didn't know. They were undoubtedly in the living room smoking crack. I sat there messing with that gun, cocking the hammer back and just being incredibly careless with a loaded gun. Sherri stood about 5 feet from me as I sat on the bed. While "playing" with this gun, I cocked the hammer back one more time and this time it went off. Now, I had shot a gun countless times before this but this time was different because this time it had gone off by accident. More importantly, the gun was pointing right at Sherri when it went off. When the gun first fired Sherri hit the ground and she just laid there. I was immediately sure that I had just accidentally shot and killed her. A couple of seconds after the shot my father hurriedly came into the room and said, "What have you done?" The woman my father was with came in the doorway of the room and started panicking when she saw Sherri lying on the floor after just hearing a gunshot. She started talking about she had to get out of there. My father quickly grabbed her and said, "You're not going anywhere." My father literally told me, "We have to kill this bitch too!" This is all happening within seconds while Sherri lie motionless on the floor. I am in a panic. I really didn't know Sherri too well yet and I was actually thinking that I should listen to my dad in this situation. The lady my dad was with started to scream when she heard what my dad told me we had to do. He grabbed her and they began to fight. I would like to think that I was not about to shoot this lady but to be honest, I'm not real sure because I did in fact pick my gun up. While we were in the middle of being about to turn an accidental shooting into a double murder, I saw Sherri move. She slowly went up to her knees and stood up. As me, my father, and the lady watched Sherri stand up we were silent and just watching. I grabbed Sherri and I hugged her. I asked her why she fell if the bullet hadn't hit her. She told me that she saw fire shoot out the barrel of the gun right in her direction and her body had just shut down. We saw the bullet hole in a door mere inches from where Sherri had been standing. The woman my dad was with called my father a few choice words and quickly left the apartment. After I realized Sherri was alright we all left. Sherri quickly forgave me. Her young mind was obviously just as ignorant as mine was. She should have left me alone that night but it was a fact that Sherri was just as crazy and lost as I was. Sometimes Sherri and I talk about this incident and we often wonder how a bullet coming out of a gun pointed right at her, missed her. I know for a fact that once again, it was God. God watching out for me for some reason. God watching over me while I took countless chances like this with my life. HE never left my side. I know that God has a bigger plan for me than what I am doing now. I belong somewhere else and doing something else. I'm going to seek out my true destiny and fulfill it. I know that God will see to it that this is done no matter what. My faith in this is growing every day.

Nov 04, 2014 7:29 AM (MF)

October 1993 Chips Townhouses...my sister had an apartment there and she sold drugs out of it. I too was selling drugs but not like my sister was. I was just making enough money each day to do or get whatever I wanted that night. When the incident that I'm about to talk about happened, my sister had moved to Alabama and I was illegally staying at the apartment she had left. It was me and about four or five of my "friends". We were all pieces of shit bound together by the stench of ignorance. During this time, I had met Sherri and brought her into this life wasting world I had started. We all would sell drugs out of the apartment and shoot our guns at the walls right in the apartment late at night. We were loud and violent every single night. We lived this way for several months and for some reason the police never showed up at my door for what we were doing. Not once. One of my friends living there with us was Louis. I believe Louis was truly a good, loyal friend even though I had just met him while I was staying at my sister's house. Louis was probably the craziest guy I had ever met. He had major mental problems that we all just summed up as being "the way everyone was". Louis was the first and only person whom I've ever seen play Russian Roulette and truly pull the trigger. Louis used to tell me how much I meant to him. I will never know why I meant so much to Louis but I can guess it was because he was hurting inside and he was reaching out for someone to show that they cared about him. I guess I was that person. Louis and I were about the same age and he was truly my friend. He had a beef with some guys who were also staying in Chips at the same time we were. He had this "beef" with these guys before I had even met him. Every day during those times I had a routine, I would smoke weed all day and when 9 PM came, I would stop smoking weed, take a shower, and begin getting drunk. I couldn't mix weed and alcohol because it made me sick so I developed this routine and I stuck to it religiously. On one night in particular I was very late beginning the part of my "routine" where I take a shower. I cannot figure out why I was so late taking a shower when I was *never* late on the "routine". I got into the shower between 10PM and 11PM that night. Every night I took a shower the apartment would be full of my "friends" and one or two crackheads acting like stray cats who won't go away because you've fed them once too often. Sherri was also there. This night, while I'm in the shower, I hear several gunshots, like 10 or so. I immediately thought they were downstairs shooting again but I knew it was way too early to be doing that. I mean I wasn't even drunk yet. I hurriedly took my shower and shut the water off and began to yell, "What the fuck is going on!?" When I stepped out the shower and grabbed my towel I went to the top of the steps to yell my question again and Sherri came running up the stairs yelling, "Clyde, they just shot Louis!" I said, "Who shot Louis?" She was so upset and scared that I could barely get the story from her. Not long after this, my friend Dave came running up the stairs saying, "They're coming in here!" I immediately went into my bedroom and grabbed my gun. I stood at the top of the steps with my gun in my hand waiting on anyone to come around that corner who didn't look familiar. I would have shot first and asked questions later. Guaranteed. Dave had run and got under a bed for some reason. After a couple of minutes of waiting, I went into my bedroom and quickly got dressed. I went downstairs and then outside. Not knowing what I would see or have to do. As I walked outside, I saw a woman holding Louis' head while sitting on the ground. He had blood coming out of his mouth and he had obviously been shot in the chest. He was unresponsive. I looked at Louis for a minute or two more and then I told Sherri to come with me. We went into the apartment and gathered all of our things up and got the hell out of there. I knew the police were coming and they were coming deep. My mother lived in the parking lot across the street from where we were and Sherri and I took our things there and then went back outside. By this time, the police and ambulance were there. Louis' parents lived right on Harmont, a minute away. When I went back down to where Louis was I saw his poor mother standing over him looking down at him. They put Louis into the ambulance and one of the officers walked up to me and asked me what happened. He said, "Do you know what happened here?" I said, "No, I was in the shower." He said, "Do you know the guy who was shot?" I said "Yeah, I know him." He said, "Well it's not looking too good for him." I found out later that Louis had shot at one of the guys he had his personal beef with and they began to have a shootout. Louis, the guy he was beefing with and one or two other people who was staying with me at the apartment had begun shooting at each other. There were bullet holes in cars and apartment windows after it was all over. Louis' wound was fatal. This incident would end our time in that apartment. Any sane person could see that something like this was bound to happen because of the way we were living. But there were no sane people there. At the time Louis was shot, I should have already been out of the shower and drunk by then. I should have been out there too. I should have been standing right beside Louis, shooting like the others were and just like Louis would have done for any of us. Everyone involved in this incident either went to prison or died. Except the guy who shot Louis. His actions were found to be in self-defense and I have no doubt that they were. Louis just didn't care. Once again, Sherri and I credit God for having me in that shower. That night I was way off of a "routine" that I had never wavered from for months before that. That night though, God did not want me out there. He wanted me here. It is incidents like this that give me the motivation to help as many people as I can. I feel in my heart that this is why God protected me. I can occasionally feel God telling me now that I'm not doing enough. He wants more out of me than I'm giving. I must put this "change" that I always talk about into overdrive. I have sacrifices to make. My friends, I have work to do.

Nov 11, 2014 7:14 AM (MF)

I was about 11 years old at the time. Now, what you need to understand is that my mother was really a very good person although sometimes she did not seem to be too fond of her own children. Sometimes she made me feel like I was a burden. I was "in the way" perhaps. At this time, she was heavily into leaving town on the truck with her married boyfriend. I remember one day in particular when she was trying to find a babysitter for me so she could leave town with him. My brother was locked up and both of my sisters were in Alabama and Florida respectively so it was just me at home at the time. My mother and father had been divorced for a while and my father was never around. Although he and I lived in the same small city, I could go months without even seeing him. My father lived like someone who was on drugs heavily. He was surrounded by prostitutes and other addicts all day every day. On this day I could hear my mother on the phone arguing with my dad about his never seeing me. I doubt she really cared whether he seen me or not. What she *really* needed was a babysitter. After she got off of the phone with him she told me to get all my stuff together. At first, I was confused. I mean, "All my stuff?" Where was I going? My mother was never the type to feel she needed to explain *anything* to a child. I gathered my few belongings and got into my mother's car with her. We drove over to my father's house and we went in. I remember this being the first time I was in my father's house. When we went in I could immediately see prostitutes and drug addicts all over the house. My father was not there at the time. I remember bringing my belongings inside the house and sitting in the kitchen. My mother told me to wait there for my dad and then she left. While I was waiting for my dad I began to think about the fact that this just might be my new home. This place was ungodly and so were the occupants. I took all of my stuff and walked into one of the bedrooms in the house. I began to set my stuff up in this bedroom like I was really moving in there. I put my clothes in a dresser and hung some up in a closet. I put the little bit of toys I had on top of the dresser. I set the bedroom up like it was my very own. Although I truly hated to be without my mother, I knew I had no choice but to stay where she told me to. After a while my father came home. I could hear him out in the living room as he was being told that my mother had brought me there and dropped me off. He came into the bedroom I was in and told me to get my stuff together. So, here I am, I just unpacked and turned this disgusting bedroom into my very own and not even an hour later, I'm packing up my stuff and about to leave again. After I packed all of my stuff up, I got into my dad's car and he began to take me home. I can remember him talking to a guy he had with him in the car about how he was about to "fuck my mom up". I don't remember him saying anything to me directly. All the way to my mom's house I was terrified at what he was about to do to my mom. He was a terrifying monster to me at that time. I barely even knew him. We finally arrive at my mom's and my only thought is that I hope she isn't home, but she was. My dad got out of the car and went into the house. I didn't know what to do and the obvious drug addict sitting in my dad's front seat was as useless to me as he probably was to whoever loved him. After a few minutes I saw my mother come running out the house. It was nighttime so I could only see her silhouette in the light but as she got closer I could see that she was *very* upset. She opened my door and said, "You're going with your father." I just looked at her. Although I didn't see him at first, my father appeared behind her and said, "No the hell he isn't." My mother turned toward him and yelled, "Yes, he is!" He then pushed her in the face so hard that she stumbled. She ran in the house and he followed her. The guy in the front seat took a drag of his cigarette and slowly said, "That's a damn shame. They arguin' over who don't want you more." Even this intoxicated, chronic drug abuser could see how wrong this was, but my parents were oblivious to it. I got out of the car, grabbed my things and walked around the house to the back porch and sat down. I felt alone. I could hear them arguing through the back door. After a little while longer my father left. I stayed home with my mother because my father had won the battle.

Fast forward to 1997. I was living in a one-bedroom trailer with Sherri and we were "behaving badly" to say the least. My first wife and I had been apart for quite a while at the time. My son CJ was 9 years old. I will admit, I didn't see my children as much as I should have when they were young. I was caught in a cycle, but even that's no excuse. Anyway, CJ was a 9-year-old bad ass kid. He was getting into major trouble in school and just not respecting anyone at all. He was on his way to join "the cycle". My ex-wife called me one day and said, "I'm about to take your son to the Detention Home." I asked why and she gave me about 10 legitimate reasons. She told me that he had to come stay with me or else. As I was about to give my excuse to why that wasn't going to happen, I suddenly remembered, I remembered what happened to me and how I felt when I knew that neither of my parents wanted me and they had no problem letting me know that. I remembered how I felt. I could not do that. I would not do that. I did not do that. I told her to get my son's stuff and I would be there to get him. I went and picked my son up. I had to change my life and that's what I did, that day. Although it was not easy, I took care of my boy. I did pretty good with very little knowledge of what being a true "father" was. I was learning on the job. We saved each other's life. I literally raised my best friend. He moved out when he was 18 and we remain best friends to this day. He is now 26 years old. I did what my father wouldn't do. My father unknowingly taught me a lesson. A lesson on what *not* to do. It is during this time with my son that I began to realize that I had a purpose, a reason to search for a better way. I began to realize that although I had little control of how my life began, it was up to me how it would end up.

Nov 17, 2014 9:50 AM

My mind has been going 100 miles per hour for days now. The last few days my mind has been taking me through several changes ranging from taking a chance and guiding my life into the unknown or keeping with the status quo perhaps for the rest of my life. I know for a fact that I am ready for a change. I know for a fact that my heart wants to branch out and attempt to reach my full potential. But I'm afraid. I'm afraid of failure. I have never really done anything majorly productive in my life and I'm beginning to doubt myself. I know that time will eventually place me where I'm supposed to be but with my being human and all, I'm continually telling myself that I can't. I have been feeling sorry for myself lately. This is a feeling that I abhor. It is a feeling that I try to avoid at all costs but sometimes it invades all corners of my mind and occupies it for a while. Perhaps social media is not the place to conduct this "pity party" but I see it like this; I am the type of person who *needs* to hear words of encouragement from people. I am also working on this flaw. "Needing" encouragement is not something that I'm proud of. I go back sometimes and read the comments some of you have written on my posts and I find them to be very encouraging. And for me, very necessary. All of my life I have felt that I have a higher calling than the cesspool that I keep swimming around in. My problem is "direction". Where to go and what to do next. I don't really have the luxury of almost unlimited time to "figure it out". I'm not a 20-year-old bright eyed kid looking forward to whatever the future holds. I am a 43-year-old man trying to open doors that I'm afraid are sealed shut now. One thing that I know with *absolute certainty* is that *I don't want to do what I've been doing*. That's *all* that I know for sure. Right now, I am lost and frankly depressed. Change is scary. Even when the change doesn't seem all that risky to some. To me, *any* change is scary. I just don't want to fail and from where I'm at and have been, failure is within reach. I keep asking myself what do I have to lose and I keep coming up with nothing. I want to be able to help people. I want to make my wife proud of me and I want to provide for her with all the effort that I can muster up because she deserves that for sticking by my side all these years which I know was no easy task. I want to be an example to those out here seeing no way other than the "wrong" way. But I'm not sure what to do. I've never been "trained" for this part of life. I was "trained" to just go out here and survive by any means necessary. And although I've become pretty good at just "surviving", I'm tired of that. On social media I have taken the book of my life and opened it up to you all so perhaps some of you can understand my confusion and doubt right now. Sometimes I read some of the posts I've written and I realize that perhaps I should be listening to my own words. It is hard for me to focus right now. My mind is all over the place. I got very little sleep last night. I kept waking Sherri up because I couldn't shake these feelings of uncertainty and doubt. I swear that I try to keep my present problems away from my friends but it is times like these that I reach out to you. I reach out to you because I know that you know how I feel. I reach out to you because I am surrounded by good, caring people who I know I can count on to raise my spirits back up and not judge me for being so very lost. I thank you for that. I know that I will find my way. Right now though, I'm lost.

Nov 21, 2014 9:12 AM

Some differences between a job and a career...

A job: living paycheck to paycheck...A career: saving for the future.

A job: an application...A career: an education.

A job: "because I *have* to"...A career: "because I *want* to"

Nov 22, 2014 9:33 AM

You Are Not Alone

You would be surprised at how many people are going through similar things that you are. Some, even worse. I have learned that while dealing with problems, it may not be enough to just "dig deep". It is not enough to just pretend everything is alright. People always talk about "haters" but the biggest "hater" resides right inside of us. I am completely aware of the fact that there are some people out here with enough confidence in themselves that they would bottle it and sell it if they could. They look at almost every tough situation as a "door" rather than a "wall". I applaud these people who have developed or have been blessed with such confidence. Some of us are still working on that but we'll get there. With a whole lot of self-reflection, I have learned a lot about myself over the past few days. I have learned that I occasionally doubt myself because after decades of mediocrity and struggle I had convinced myself that this is not only the way it is, but this is the way it's supposed to be. And any attempt to disrupt this hopeless flow would result in feelings of failure and self-loathing. I was looking into the eyes of my fellow have-nots and mistaking their confusion at what I was saying for doubt. They weren't "doubting" what I was saying, they were just confused by it because I was talking about achieving things that seem to work out for "other" people but not us. They look like they're thinking, "Clyde, what are you talking about? That's not how we do things here." Trust me when I tell you this, few are humbler than me, but I must say that I have built enough confidence in myself to realize that I am a pretty special person. I am no victim. I believe that I am a born leader and a warrior. I am a good friend and a faithful husband. I am strong both mentally and physically. I am smart. I possess both common and good sense. I feel compassion for those in need of it and I would give up half of my last dollar to feed someone who is also hungry. I am a fighter. These are all things that I already know about myself. No one can convince me that any of these things are not true. I have realized that with hard work and dedication, there is *nothing* that I want to do that I cannot do. Nothing. My eyes have seen a lot. My ears have heard a lot. But not enough. My eyes and ears have seen and heard things that had me convinced that I had reached the "end of the road" as far as being truly happy goes. I *let* them convince me of that. I let the repetition of hopelessness convince me of that. I used to exude confidence all the time but *that* confidence was superficial. It was an act. It was me constantly telling others that "their life doesn't have to be the way it is", while knowing that if I were to face what they are facing, I'd crumble too. I'd cry too. I'd give up too. It has always been so easy for me to tell someone else exactly how they should handle almost any situation. Easy until that someone became "me". In order for me to believe what I was telling myself, I not only had to dig deep, but I had to change the whole way that I thought about myself. I'm not living the life I'm living because I *have* to. I am living the life I'm living because I have been convinced that my feet are set in this concrete of being an average "struggler". Convinced by whom? Convinced by life. In the past in my life, I would walk up to the ever so tall "wall of doubt", look up, and then turn around and take my place back among the hopeless where I belonged. I have once again walked up to that wall but this time is different. This time I have a ladder of confidence. This wall is becoming less intimidating to me. I have planted the seeds of confidence within myself and I am nurturing them now. I fully expect them to grow and flourish. It won't happen overnight and I realize that there will undoubtedly be setbacks. I must recognize them as temporary and carry on. With all the strength and self-confidence, I can muster, I *must* carry on. I can give those whom I intend on helping all kinds of stories about what I've been through but with these stories of trials and tribulations there must be a "happy ending". An "ending" that says, "Nothing is given except the ability to earn". My friends, I know there are so many of us with our own personal problems that frankly embarrass and weigh on us. Especially when we think about how our personal problems look through the eyes of the "judgmental". Those who hide *their* embarrassing problems while pointing at yours. Caring what these people say or think will only exacerbate the original problem. It seems that some people were put on this earth just to doubt you. And *not* caring about what they think is sometimes easier said than done. Anyone can tell you that you're smart or pretty or a hard worker or give you any number of complements, but unless you can tell yourself these things and wholeheartedly believe it, their words mean practically nothing in the grand scheme of things. Regardless if a hater tells you that you "can't" do something or if a supporter tells you that you "can" do something, it all boils down to what you yourself believe. Do you believe in yourself? Because if you don't, don't expect someone else to simply place that belief within you. It doesn't work that way. Believing in yourself comes from the inside out. It has to. I used to put all kinds of credence into compliments that people gave me, until I stood at that "wall of doubt" and all I had was those complements and I realized that no matter how many compliments I got, I could not use them to conquer this wall standing in front of me. Complements are merely words. Well intended words. But still just words nonetheless. Perhaps a complement can spark a fire within you that lets you know that "something" is there but it is impossible to get over that "wall" on complements alone. After going back and reading I see that from the very first post I ever wrote on social media up to this one right here, I've let complements and superficial confidence get me to the base of the "wall" but there was nothing there to get me over it or even help me begin to climb it. Part of winning the battle is realizing what is holding back your ability to "conquer".

Understanding that, *nothing* worth having will be given to you. It is no one else's job to make you feel content with your own choices. No one is entitled to happiness and the feeling of good self-worth. People rarely see "your" struggle as "their" struggle although sometimes the struggles are almost identical yet they are just being handled in different ways because we all have our own ways of standing up to universal upheavals. For example, most of us live paycheck to paycheck and that in itself is a problem but whether some choose to spend their little bit of money on food or weed or partying or bills, the commonality remains, "living paycheck to paycheck". Same problem, different brains handling them.

I will keep you updated on my progress as I continue to stand up to the "wall of doubt". My successes *and* my failures will be no secret. The ebb and flow of my confidence and self-worth will not be hidden from you. If and when I do succeed at getting over that wall, may my life be a blueprint to others who will still be standing on the other side of it waiting on someone to toss them a rope that may never come. One day I will be able to look a lost, struggling soul in their eyes and say, "I was where you are and now I am here to help you get to where you need to be." God Bless my friends.

Nov 26, 2014 8:22 PM

When the devil tries to convince you that your life is so bad, before you believe him, make sure you talk to God first. There must be beautiful clouds above me right now because it is raining blessings. GOD IS GOOD PEOPLE! GOD IS SO GOOD!!!!!!!!!

Nov 26, 2014 9:01 PM

Happy Thanksgiving to each and every one of you. I know there are some things happening in our world that are dividing us but Thanksgiving isn't about arguing about what's right and what's wrong, it is about *being thankful.* It is about walking through your day finding things to smile about and realizing that although you may have things to frown about, not now, not on Thanksgiving. On this day we will laugh with and enjoy our families. And for those of us who have to work, we will laugh with and enjoy our friends. We will spend time appreciating. Appreciating that wonderful person who worked for hours making that feast. Appreciating life as you hug wonderful people you haven't seen in a while. Just saturating ourselves in appreciation all day. We will pray for those who need it and give our time to those who want it. Happy Thanksgiving my friends.

Dec 02, 2014 10:53 AM

If you're just walking around all day every day with a shitty attitude just for no reason other than you just don't care how anyone else feels and you choose to give even strangers healthy doses of your crappie attitude just because you are a terrible person just acting like the world owes you, if this is you then I've got two words for you.... Fuck (and) You!!!!!

Dec 04, 2014 6:27 AM

No matter what the subject is, just because someone has a different opinion than yours, doesn't make them wrong. It's an *opinion*. Treating your own opinion like it's a fact makes *you* wrong.

Dec 08, 2014 7:42 AM (MF)

Child Support

I sit and I wait...right outside my front door

He said he was coming but he's said that before

But this time feels different...this time he just might

That belief can't be taken from me for I hold it too tight

It's a little past the time but maybe he's just lost

Maybe he was with someone...and had to drop them off

God forbid he's been hurt and I just don't know yet

Yesterday I told him I'd be ready...he hasn't had time to forget

Maybe he's just mad at my mom and I should walk up the street

But I told him I'd be waiting right here...right here in this very seat

In a minute I'll call him to see if he's still at home

I call and I call...still no answer...something must be wrong with his phone

It's been an hour now...he's running really late

He must have forgotten where I'm at...I'll call him just in case

I called him three more times and left a message once

He's probably saying right now..." I have to go get my son."

My friends want my company but they don't understand

They have no idea why I can't move from right where I am

He's two hours tardy and I'm starting to get worried

The day is growing shorter...my father had better hurry

I ask my mother if he's coming or did he tell a lie

She tries to reassure me but I see truth in her eyes

I bow my head in sadness and I go back to my seat

It's been three hours now and I'm convinced...he's forgotten about me

I'll bet he doesn't love me...I'll bet he doesn't even care

The internal pain from his lies is almost more than I can bear

One day he'll want *my* time...not remembering what he did with his

That day I'll show him what being heartbroken is

One day I'll make him sit on a porch and wait for me to arrive

He'll have tears in his eyes when he realizes that I too can lie

He'll ask my mom where I'm at and his heart will fill with hate

He'll see one day that it's not me...it is HIM who is the mistake

I love my father...maybe more than I should...I wonder if he knows

My love and forgiveness is wearing thin as my all out hatred grows

So here I sit upon this porch waiting for this night to end

I'm so heartbroken and disappointed...but tomorrow I'll wait again

Dec 11, 2014 6:26 AM

The "old" definition of racism: the belief that one race is inferior or superior to another race or races. The "new" definition of racism: if two different races disagree on *anything* ever. So sad.

Dec 12, 2014 9:21 AM

Did you know that...

1) I don't develop emotional attachments to "things".

2) Sometimes embarrassment causes me to lie.

3) I haven't had a headache in years.

4) Back in the 80's I thought I was Prince.

5) My mother once told me that she was afraid to die.

6) It is hard for me to "pretend" to like someone.

7) I sleep with my light on at night.

8) I have a very short attention span.

9) I very rarely dream.

10) I love to separate and count change.

11) My legs are freakishly skinny.

12) My wife and I sleep in two different bedrooms.

13) I don't eat steak or roast.

14) I am afraid to touch living fish.

15) I will stop any cat from licking its own crotch.

16) I don't do weddings or funerals or graveyards.

17) I hate watching movies.

18) I think tongue kissing is disgusting.

19) I pissed the bed one time as an adult.

20) I take medication every day that I can't live without.

21) I have no pictures of people on my walls.

22) I am afraid to look at a possum.

23) I wear underwear and boxers at the same time.

24) I hate sleeping and I wish I never had to do it.

25) My mother's father was a racist.

26) Rollercoasters bore me.

27) I am not comfortable without a shirt on.

28) I don't tell people that I love them...even if I do.

29) I find it easy to admit when I'm obviously wrong.

30) I am addicted to knowing what time it is.

31) I type with two fingers.

32) I dropped out of college three times.

32 1/2) I rarely finish what I start.

33) I have a soft heart for the elderly.

34) I have no problem with crying.

35) Sometimes I judge people by how white their socks are.

36) I am the king of overreacting.

37) When I'm home alone...I sometimes pace for long periods of time.

38) Although I felt it all the time as a kid, I rarely feel lonely as an adult.

39) I truly dislike having company at my house.

40) I love my wife more than I've ever loved anyone in my life and if her and I were the last two people on earth...I could still die happy.

41) I don't touch public door knobs.

42) If I smell your fart...I will hate you a little.

43) I have never worn a suit as an adult. Unless a tuxedo is a suit.

44) I wish there was no such thing as nighttime.

45) I used to have five holes in each of my ears.

46) I am incredibly impatient.

47) When I met Sherri...she had a nose ring.

48) I hate wearing new clothes.

49) If I find a hair in my food I will think and gag about it for hours.

50) I am turned off by white girls who "act black".

Dec 18, 2014 7:44 AM

My enemy's friend is also my enemy. That's just life.

Dec 19, 2014 5:44 PM

When I was in my 20's, I should have used some common sense and got ready for my 40's which would have set me up for my 60's. As it is, I blew my 20's and I get ready for my 40's *in* my 40's which causes me to neglect the set up for my 60's. Oh well, it is what it is.

Dec 20, 2014 12:14 PM

Whoever says "money can't buy happiness" is underestimating the power of money. Money can buy *anything*. Even a longer life. Quit your job and say, "To hell with *anything* that I need money for", and watch your happiness soar.

Dec 22, 2014 6:06 AM

Christmas isn't supposed to be depressing. Don't let lack of materials ruin your spirit. Don't let yourself be convinced that the best you could do, is not good enough. Your very best is *always* good enough. Although we can't touch love, we can certainly feel it. Love, it's all I want for Christmas and I already have plenty and so do you. Merry Christmas my friends.

Dec 23, 2014 7:07 AM

Dudes who are goin' bald on top but still got a ponytail refuse to quit. It's "out of business" in the front and "still partying" in the back.

Dec 24, 2014 11:48 AM

Very little in this world is more disgusting than a public restroom. If you get up from a toilet and there is a "streak" on the back of the toilet, you are in need of some serious hygiene counseling. You are gross and you probably stink. Merry Christmas Stinky.

Dec 30, 2014 12:26 PM

As 2014 comes to a close I have been pondering where I'm at in some aspects of life. My debts, be they financial or emotional, are being paid by *me*. They are not being ignored. Financially, I am still paying some of the debts I made when I was in my 20's and thinking I'll never see my 30's. Child support, hospital bills, IRS, City of Canton, and more. They have all taken a huge chunk of my life away from me and I deserved every bit of it. I never looked for a handout. I worked my ass off for every dime I owed and paid. Emotionally, I've realized over the past couple of years that I've hurt people whom I don't even remember hurting. There have been times when I was talking to someone whom I have not seen in a very long time and I don't even remember that they hate me. I usually remember after some reflection about that person. I have emotionally hurt (in some cases devastated) several women in my past. They knew that cold hearted piece of

189

shit who didn't care about anyone. Who they may not know is this remorseful person sitting before you who often reminisces and regrets his behavior toward them. I don't like when people think about me and the thought is that of some sort of pain. No matter who it is. My wife often tells me to "just give it to the Lord" and perhaps this is possible. But for my own peace of mind, I must feel the remorse and grief of hurtful deeds from the past. I need to feel it. I deserve to feel it. I *want* to feel it. Believe it or not it actually helps me be a better person. It helps me be faithful to my wife, because I owe it. It helps me give a complete stranger half of my last, because I owe it. It helps me give respect to *every* man, because I owe it. It helps me have the ability to talk to a young man about his future and he is genuinely taking in *all* I am saying. It helps me seek out those who are upset and try to comfort them. However, I am faithful to my wife mostly because I love her but you get my point. These are just some of the ways that I pay my emotional debts. I have a few dreams that I want to make come true before I die and one of the most important to me is to leave this world *totally* debt free. Emotionally and financially. Although I am aware of the fact that God could handle this for me, I prefer to handle this myself. So, my New Year's resolution will be the same as it was last year, to continue to work on these debts. Happy New Year my friends!

2015

Jan 08, 2015 5:22 PM

I believe the true essence of being a leader is not getting a kick out of "bossing" people around, it is the feeling you get knowing that they want to do what you ask because you've earned their respect.

Jan 12, 2015 9:53 AM

I feel so happy and content right now and for no particular reason. My worries are down and my hope is up. I know this could change any minute so I want to take advantage of this feeling for as long as I can. I still have "problems" but they are the kind of problems that I can easily handle and for that I'm thankful. Sure, things could be "better" but I'm incredibly satisfied with them being just "okay" right now. I don't have that worried feeling in my stomach or that situation that tries to squash any happiness just by thinking about it. Today, *right now* in my life, I'm okay. I pray that most of you are at least "okay" right now. This morning, I searched for my blessings and began to dwell on them. There are too many to count. God, how I wish that I could feel this way forever. Perhaps I cannot, but at least for today...

At least for today

My problems have gone away

Where they're at...I hope they stay

It's rainy and cold on this beautiful day

Still I smile and feel compelled to say...

Keep me hopeful...oh Lord I pray

Good morning my friends. Here's to your day being filled with enough hope to fuel positive results for tomorrow and forever.

Jan 13, 2015 5:37 PM

Whoever I meet and get to know, one of my main goals with that person is to see to it that they never forget me for the rest of their life and that those memories contain feelings that force a smile. Real talk.

Jan 17, 2015 9:37 AM

Nonsense is for people with no sense and a lot of time on their hands. I'm practicing spotting nonsense immediately and acting accordingly. Nonsense is a waste of time that I don't have to waste.

Jan 18, 2015 4:13 PM

Sometimes I think that we as parents have no idea how much our children really love us. We know they love us but to what extent is sometimes surprising. My children love me perhaps more than they should and for that I will *always* have something to feel absolutely blessed about. I mean, even me, my mother could not possibly have known how much she truly meant to me and how much pure love I had and still have for her.

Jan 20, 2015 6:54 AM

Sometimes I can hear Father Time talking to me. "Clyde, it's getting late."

Jan 28, 2015 1:04 PM

If you can look into the face of disappointment and sorrow and remain focused on the fact that it is so very temporary in the grand scheme of life, then I envy you. If your heart has the ability to make you genuinely smile even when your mind is screaming, "Be angry", "Be vengeful", "Be hateful", "Be disappointed", then I envy you. I know that temporary setbacks should never impede upon permanent goals. I know that life is not about "the moment" as much as it is about the entire journey. If you know these things and being happy and content is something you never have to force, then I envy you. I know some people who are like this and it has nothing to do with religion or money. It is their heart. It is the fact that they've reached bliss even without being ignorant. They inspire me to keep trying to let my heart dictate my behavior and attitude, not my circumstances or any one moment. I may not always be able to control what my heart and mind take in, but I know I can control what I put out. I'm just sick of being angry and feeling vengeful for the things other people say or do. I need to stop confusing "forgiving" someone with just being too "weak" to "defend" myself. I need to get better at differentiating situations that call for "defense" and ones that call for "forgiveness". Not every volatile situation needs my anger, some need my understanding. I'm working on it.

I'm hard at work on being one of those whom I envy. I know I will get there simply because I belong there.

Jan 28, 2015 1:58 PM

Sometimes we hurt the ones we love and expect complete and timely forgiveness. Not realizing that the loved one we hurt has to "give" us forgiveness. Forgiveness can't just be "taken" from someone. All that trying to "take" forgiveness from someone will do is make you need more forgiveness. If you're seeking someone's forgiveness, don't try to obtain it by force. Once you show and tell them how much their forgiveness means to you, it is out of your hands. Unfortunately for you, all you can do is wait and hope that they see you as someone worthy of their precious forgiveness.

Jan 28, 2015 2:40 PM

If you seem to have some sort of problem with damn near everybody you know, perhaps damn near *everybody* else ain't the problem.

Jan 28, 2015 2:43 PM

Change can be growth.

Jan 28, 2015 2:49 PM

I believe God gives us the "tools" to do it. The motivation is part of free will and therefore *ours* to get.

Jan 29, 2015 10:55 AM

Roads so slippery they make you turn your radio off and focus.

Jan 30, 2015 6:58 PM

Backstabbing should be punishable by a legal ass whooping. Backstabbers are mentally slow and have no shame. They are confusing to me.

Jan 31, 2015 10:07 AM

We all know someone like this. If you don't know anyone like this, just remember, these type of people do not have the ability to step outside of themselves and honestly look at themselves. Maybe you don't know anyone like this because it just may be *you*...

I should be able to do and say whatever I want and not have to worry about any type of retaliation or consequence. Even if I don't show respect, I still expect it.

Whether I earn or not, I deserve. I *love* pointing out problems although I have absolutely *no* desire to offer even one real solution. If it's not important to me, then it's not important. If it *is* important to me then nothing else matters. My two favorite words in the English language is "I" and "me". Unless I'm in a conflict with someone, then my favorite word becomes "you". If I get into an argument with you, *all* I will remember is what *you* said. Anything I said will be "justified" by my inability to care how I make others feel. I am very very rarely wrong and when I am obviously wrong, I will get angry if we don't immediately move on. I *do not* apologize. There is never any reason for me to apologize. I mean, for what? I didn't do anything. If a situation comes up that requires an apology from me then obviously, it's someone else's fault. I will not adjust to situations. Situations *must* adjust to me and if they don't, well, I don't understand that and I lash out and begin blaming others because how could I be wrong? The word "effort" does not mean the same to me as it does to most people. To me it means, no matter how much effort I'm giving, it's enough. It must be enough because I'm giving a little bit of effort and I'm me. If you don't like the way I am then allow me to show you how quickly I can move on from people who won't just deal with the way I am. I don't mind saying GOODBYE.

Jan 31, 2015 1:55 PM

It takes the blink of an eye to cause a permanent change. Be that change good or bad. It takes but a moment to realize life will never be the same.

Feb 05, 2015 5:45 AM

Sherri McCrae...you are my wife and my best friend. We have fought through countless tribulations and we end up in each other's arms after every one. Our relationship is unstoppable. Anyone who knows us, knows that. I love you ten times more than any proof I could ever show. Maybe twenty. Happy Anniversary Mrs. McCrae.

Feb 05, 2015 5:44 PM

Strength to overcome *anything* comes from within. You, me, we all have reserved strength. It's just about locating it and believing in the power it possesses. Let time run its course. Your time will eventually be due. Find that strength within you and use it until "due time". Hang in there. We all suffer and we all have the strength to push forward. Find yours, and use it. Giving up is *NOT AN OPTION*.

Feb 07, 2015 12:14 AM

Although she spent most of her life alone, she never acted lonely. I wonder if she was. I'm just missing my mother tonight.

Feb 08, 2015 7:36 AM

Did you know that there are women out here who literally go to school, work a job and take care of their children? They do this routine almost every day. They are machines whose sacrifices will eventually pay off. They have no excuses. Your tears are looked upon as necessary venting within a life such as yours. Your smile, although sometimes forced, is your temporary reward for your significant sacrifices. Your "permanent" reward will be the example you've set for your children. Your children are learning the difference between "waiting on it" and "going to get it". Your example to your children is immeasurable. We all know that it would be so much easier to be some sorry dumb bitch out here using your little bit of government money to cater to some dude whose only mission in life is to "collect and sell scrap". Their daughters seeing a different dude all up in Mommy's bedroom every other weekend. Their sons learning from these morons, learning that life is all about being lazy and unproductive and if there is no shortcut then there must be an excuse.

I applaud you hardworking ladies. You all need to post your routines and sacrifices on social media every day for all the women out here with lame excuses and even worse, a lame man whose definition of taking care of business is making his girl take care of him. Yeah, that's right, I called you a lame. I know you're a lame because many years ago, I was you and I was a lame.

God bless the mother who sacrifices every day for the wellbeing of her child. Your pedestal is shining and no lame man or sorry bitch can get you off of it.

Feb 10, 2015 10:53 AM

In my 20's I thought that I knew nothing else. In my 30's I began to notice that maybe "this" isn't someone else's fault. I was never really "lazy" per se but there is no doubt that I lacked structure and discipline. And probably basic respect for our whole world be it human, animal or property. I felt angry all the time but I could never really pinpoint where it was originating from. Who exactly was I angry with? Everyone in my life? Because that's who I was lashing out at. Am I angry with strangers? Because that's who I'm lashing out at. Am I angry with animals? Because they too are who I'm lashing out at. Was it even anger I felt or was it perhaps something else? Maybe something more complicated than that. Was it the fact that almost everyone around me was doing the same things? Was I a "follower" or was I being followed? When I would do something awful to someone or something I would often wonder afterwards how everyone else dealt with the overwhelming remorse. Personally, I would replace it with more awful deeds. It was a cycle of "deeds" and remorse, "deeds" and remorse. At the time, I dare not speak of my remorseful feelings to anyone because with all certainty, it would be considered "soft" and that's *not* what you want to be considered as. So I went on with life piling up awful memories in my cycle of deeds and remorse. Not only memories but feelings I would feel obligated to atone for later on in life. Why did I keep doing it even though every fiber in my being was telling me not to? Why did I feel so obligated to look more ruthless than I really was? If it was in fact the people who I was hanging around, then why was I around them? Why was I so drawn to them? Did I have an addiction to feeling remorseful? Remorse is sometimes a necessary feeling but more often than not, a bad feeling. How can I be addicted to something that I loathed feeling? I doubt any of us really wanted to be there. Well, maybe one or two of us were *really* crazy and genuinely dangerous. I was "dangerous" but not because I wanted to be and I don't know why I was other than the fact that I chose to be. I chose that even though I had other choices. Why? Why would I make such a choice? Was I so oblivious to my future that I would all but ruin it with terrible conscious decisions? I truly believe that in most cases, geography is destiny and children imitate their atmosphere. In a lot of ways, we subconsciously turn into our parents. Personally, I would eventually recognize what my subconscious was up to and I consciously steered in a different direction. It is but by the GRACE OF GOD that I recognized it before it took me out completely. There are a lot of young people out here who are feeling the way I felt, who have questions similar to the ones I had. They need to be told that *all* you have to do is make a different choice. *That is all*. You're giving up on life because it seems as if those around you have. I sometimes question whether I was a leader or a follower because, actually, we were going nowhere. And who needs to be lead to nowhere? We were just running around waiting on that one "awful deed" that would seal the deal on our futures. It was all about choices then, and it's all about choices now. *Decisions. Conscious decisions.* Believe me when I tell you, how you grew up is no reason for a bad *decision*. Who you hang with, how seriously you take your education, how you treat people, these are all decisions that are yours. They belong to no one else. *You* make them. So when it's all said and done you should continuously ask yourself one question; "Who is responsible for the decisions I make?", and then honestly answer it. Eventually, you will realize that *your* bad decisions not only affect you but they affect those you profess to love. Those whose only crime was loving you and caring enough to let *your* bad decisions affect them. They are victims of *your* bad decisions. Shame on you. Shame on you for giving up on yourself when those you love still believe in you. They are at least worthy of a second or third thought before you make that bad decision. It doesn't have to be this way. I promise you, *nothing* in your life is more important than your very own *decisions*.

Feb 11, 2015 8:54 AM

Four years ago today I walked out of my boss' office with a nice promotion under my belt. After I left his office I was feeling accomplished and proud and I couldn't wait to tell Sherri. As I walked out about to go home, my mother calls me. I answer it anticipating telling her about my brand new promotion.

Me: Hello?

Mom: How are you doing?

Me: Great. I was just promoted.

Mom: That's very good son. I'm proud of you.

Me: Thanks mom.

Mom: Well I have some bad news.

Me: What happened?

Mom: Your father just died.

Me: God, please don't do this.

Mom: I'm sorry son. I love you.

Me: I love you too Mom. Goodbye.

This was the very first time that I had someone this close to me pass away. At that moment, I felt an overwhelming sense of grief. Almost like it was difficult to breathe. I go outside and get into the car with Sherri and she could immediately tell something was wrong. After I got into the car, I just let it go. I began to cry harder than I ever did as an adult. My soul had never been so controlled by sadness. My father spent most of his life battling his very powerful demons. So much time in fact that he had very little time for anything else. I never got to tell him much about how I truly felt about him. I regret that. It's easy to say, "He knew how I felt. " But I doubt he did. We are all missing you today Old Man. Today and forever more.

Feb 12, 2015 7:25 PM

Sometimes I confuse someone having a bad day with being mad at me personally. I hate when I do that. I'm trying to get better at recognizing it.

Feb 18, 2015 7:17 AM

Sure, we have our problems. Sometimes we argue about dumb stuff. Sometimes we need to be away from each other for a moment or two. But no matter what, I mean no matter the circumstances, within our relationship we both trust. We have wholehearted trust for each other. Our complete loyalty to each other is unwavering. I would *never* allow another woman to hurt my wife through me. There is not a woman on earth capable of coming in between the bond we have. There are *no* secrets, no cell phones being locked and we both have always had each other's passwords be it social media or anything else. My wife knows exactly where I'm at 24 hours a day, 7 days a week, 365 days a year. Not because she "needs" to know but because there are absolutely no barriers between her and even the most intimate parts of my life. I "want" her to know. Years ago, I found her worthy of entrusting my heart to her and she has done nothing but love and take care of it. It is *truly* "until death do us part" in our world. She is responsible for at least 90% of my happiness. This kind of loving bond takes practice, sacrifice and sometimes compromise and forgiveness. Each of which we do daily. Loyalty is the key. Loyalty is the glue that holds this together. Without loyalty, there would be no "us". Us...me and Sherri, forever connected in something *no* outside source could ever penetrate with the temptation of disloyalty. We are forever bonded by mutual respect, loyalty, and the truest sense of the word love and all it's beautiful meaning. I love you Sherri McCrae.

Feb 18, 2015 8:12 AM

I really hate when I'm walking into a public place and someone holds the door for me when I'm like 30 feet away. They make you have to run to get there so you're not being rude. Sometimes I stop and turn around until they give up.

Feb 21, 2015 12:39 PM

I can remember when I was a kid we loved the snow. We would stay outside for hours and hours just playing football. I never got sick from it. I don't see kids out anywhere in weather like this these days. Lazy ass kids would rather play football with a game controller than an actual football.

Mar 02, 2015 6:14 PM

Call me crazy but I think folks who think their freedom is worth a little bit of fast money are fools. In fact, I *know* it. A nice car, nice clothes, even a new house, how can any of that be worth even one day of your freedom? Most of the time the police are going to take all of your shit anyway when those "consequences" come calling. You willingly go from a so-called "baller" to a definite "burden". A burden on those who care about you so they have to deal with the consequences *you* chose to face and take care of you while you're in prison. You become a financial and emotional burden on your loved ones by choice. Although I truly realize that working your ass off for a few hundred dollars a week sounds crazy too, I swear you'll never go to prison for it. Perhaps I'll never be a "baller", but with that comes the fact that I'll never be a burden. I work hard for the little bit that I have and *no one* will ever take it from me. You fools had better wake up. Life ain't as easy as you're trying to make it. The law will prove that to you. Foolish future burdens.

Mar 03, 2015 9:38 AM (MF)

The arrest itself will be maybe the most terrible ordeal you have ever gone through. You will probably get your ass kicked by the police. The charges, the indictment, the sentence, and although living through that will suck, it can't compare to the loneliness that being locked up provides. Is your girl out fucking some other dude after you're not allowed on the phone for the night? Is someone who you love going to pass away while you're doing time? "Why ain't nobody answering my calls?" "My visits were frequent at first but now it seems as if I'm out of sight... out of mind" You're going to learn what it's like to be around dozens of people and still be sick with loneliness. The most important time of the day is getting mail. Will you be getting any? Maybe, at first you will. Maybe. The stinking van rides to court, the disrespectful judge, your uninterested public defender, the awful food, the confinement, the loneliness, the hopelessness, they all bring the tears. Privacy, GONE! Genuine happiness, GONE! Freedom, GONE! Coitus, GONE! A stainless steel cold toilet or a disgusting shower, that's where you get your "alone" time and even then you have to just pretend you're alone, because you're not. The constant physical threats will weigh heavily on your already fragile psyche. But when it's all said and done, you will just be dealing with consequences that you yourself *chose* to face. You have become *nothing* but a mere burden. If you think even one of these consequences is worth it then perhaps you truly belong in prison. Foolish burden. You'd better wake up and smell the coffee. Life ain't that easy. Don't be a pathetic burden.

Mar 05, 2015 5:52 AM

I've realized that everyone I've ever really needed in my life resides right inside of me. These are the only people I truly can count on, the only people who, if they betray me or let me down, it is totally my own fault.

Mar 11, 2015 9:10 PM

The very first thing that attracted me to her was that she was so very beautiful but didn't seem to know it. She truly doesn't even know how to think she is better than anyone else.   Sherri McCrae

Mar 14, 2015 8:25 PM

You just walk around like your shit don't stink

I hate the way you eat...I hate the way you drink

You lie there all day...just blinking all slow

You piss me off all the time and somehow I think you know

You sneak up beside me and out of nowhere you attack

I'm getting to the point where I'm going to bite you back

You bully my dog and it makes me mad that he won't stand his ground

You think that you're scaring ME when you make those stupid sounds

You're always so damn angry with a shitty attitude

You don't want me in my bedroom when you're in a pissy mood

You're only safe because the lady of the house has your back

I "dislike" a lot of things but God I *hate* my wife's cat

Mar 15, 2015 5:12 PM

Within the body of an opportunist beats the heart of a coward. To be so heartless as to take the life of someone merely because you want what they have, that's a special kind of cowardice. I believe it is time to start calling these fools what they are, cowardice scum. They run around our community hurting and taking the lives of our family and friends, and for what? To prove how "hard" they are? Putting a gun in someone's face and taking what they have is bad enough, but pulling the trigger and ending his life, the only thing that should earn you is a special place in hell. How dare you. You should have been aborted. Even your own mother knows that you should have been aborted. You care nothing about the pain and heartache you cause. You have no conscious. And for that, you should have been aborted. We are tired of this. We are tired of cowardice scum who don't even deserve to breathe our air hurting and taking the lives of our loved ones. We're done making excuses for you bastards. We're done blaming your behavior on your upbringing. We will blame it on *you*. Solely on you. We are tired of this. We are tired of your cowardice decisions causing us fear and pain. We are tired of the worry you fill our minds with. Earlier, I was talking to my son and he said to me, "Dad, even if *you* took someone's life just to take what they have, I would disown you." All his statement made me feel was, relief. I was relieved by the fact that he sees the absolute evil in doing something like that. I was relieved while still being cognizant of the fact that one of these evil cowards could choose to take him from me or me from him. Much love and prayers to the family and friends of that young man. He obviously had an incredible amount of love in our community. I personally pray that God swiftly exacts the vengeance we all feel in our hearts on whomever it was that Satan himself sent into this world to take this young man's life. *WE ARE TIRED OF THIS.*

Mar 16, 2015 8:00 AM

With *all* due respect and I'm not talking about anyone in particular, but going to prison is *not* an accomplishment nor does it make you "hard". If anything, *not* going to prison is an accomplishment.

Mar 17, 2015 10:16 AM

Sometimes it is truly alright to regroup, reinvent and restart. That does not mean "giving up". It means "moving on". It means acknowledging speed bumps are not walls. There is no need to uncontrollably "run" from the past. You have plenty of time to remain under control and "walk" away. The past is stationary. The past doesn't follow you unless you drag it along. Let it go, regroup, reinvent and restart. We owe it to ourselves.

Mar 18, 2015 7:39 AM

Hitting a pothole will make a devout Christian yell, "FUCK!"

Mar 20, 2015 4:57 AM

I'm not real sure why, but some people consciously choose embarrassment over effort.

Mar 20, 2015 6:17 PM

I think the world would be a better place if everyone would just curse all the time. I will never stop cursing. People try to pretend like they don't curse, but they curse. And it's probably funny. Okay, children cursing isn't funny. But elderly people cursing is. One day I was behind a huge ass Cadillac Brougham and I couldn't see a driver. The car was in the turning lane *and* the going straight lane at the same time. The light turned green and the car moved up about 5 feet and just sat there. No blinker or any indication of what it was about to do. So I'm like, "What the hell?" I pull up beside the car and I see the tiniest old lady who could barely see out the car's door window. I stop beside the car and I yell, "You shouldn't be driving!" This old lady who had to be every day of 90 years old looks over at me and all I could see was from the top of her old lady glasses up. She slowly tilts her head straight up so I could see her mouth and she screams, "Fuck you!" She slowly put her head back to where I could only see from her eyes up again and then I see her frail middle finger come up from the door at an alarmingly slow rate. It was crooked and shaking and had a big ass piece of costume jewelry on it. She even lowered it slowly. After I took in all the slow shit that had just happened, I busted out laughing. Don't tell me cursing can't make a situation better.

Mar 21, 2015 9:17 AM

Some people want me to accept them for "who they are", but what about accepting *me* for not liking who you are?

Mar 22, 2015 9:16 AM

I wonder if it's possible to love someone yet not want to be around them or talk to them even though you're not mad at them at all. Perhaps with emotions, the possibilities are endless.

Mar 23, 2015 4:55 AM

To me, women physically fighting is extremely unattractive. Women punching each other in the face is just tacky under *any* circumstance.

Mar 29, 2015 7:26 AM

The drive of all I can possibly accomplish today is on "FULL" this morning. I will see to it today that tonight when I finally lie down to rest, I will be resting assured that I gave this day *every* positive ounce of my being. I will see to it that this "full" tank of drive that I have this morning is on "empty" by tonight. The drive to thrive is alive and palpable today!

Apr 03, 2015 3:27 PM

People be arguing and hurting each other over the dumbest shit. I know a dude who is constantly getting his ass kicked because he is constantly defending his sister's "honor". His sister gets punched in the eye a lot by her boyfriend. Women should always interview the ex-girlfriend (who will most likely be *more* than honest) about what she went through before she "falls in love". The new girlfriend should ask questions like...

"Are you two still together?"

"Did he ever beat your ass?"

"How many kids does he really have?"

"What's his job situation?"

"Does he come home at night?"

"Does he have other girlfriends?"

You could save yourself a lot of heartache with an "interview". A guy can't have that interview. The last thing a guy wants to do is talk to his girlfriend's ex about *anything*. We *hate* that dude. (or in most cases, "those dudes") Women might hate the ex too but women can tolerate more shit than most men can. I *know* this to be true. Women can find out you've been cheating and hold that shit in as long as they want to. Men react immediately. A woman can listen to you tell a big ass lie and she knows you're lying and she will pretend she believes you for as long as she wants to. Women are good at bad surprises. They're really enviable abilities.

Anyway, that guy just keeps getting his ass beat every time his sister takes one to the eye from the same guy who *keeps* punching her in the eye. It's like she thinks he has gotten all of the "eye punching" out of his system this time. But he's always got more. Her *and* her brother walk around with black eyes and bruises from this girl's boyfriend. Silly adult humans.

Apr 07, 2015 6:32 AM

Just get out there and *try*. Your life is just sitting at a green light. Hit the gas and GO! You probably can't reach it because you're sitting down waiting on something to fall into your lap. Stand up and be about something. What are you waiting on? Seriously, what the hell are you waiting on?

Apr 12, 2015 6:23 AM

The amount of respect you demand; is the amount of respect you deserve. Perhaps they continually disrespect you simply because they can. People can only take advantage of you with your permission.

Apr 17, 2015 11:56 AM

Do you know someone who is such a terrible human being that you find it almost impossible to believe that *anyone* in the world cares about them? Just somebody who is out to cause as much misery as they can. I know someone like that. She's ugly, inside and out.

Apr 18, 2015 8:00 PM

God,

When I die...I'll die with sins and doubt

Yet and still...I pray that I die from the inside out

Let it not be by poison, by gun nor by knife

Although I must die...let no mere man take my life

Amen

Apr 21, 2015 12:29 PM

If they're hurting you, physically and/or mentally, and still saying that they love you, use some common sense. One thing I know for sure my friend, is that love doesn't hurt. Love doesn't demean you or cheat on you or beat on you. Love is healthy, strong and supportive and *always* ready to team up with you and face *any* adversarial situation head on. Love doesn't hurt. Only pain does. Perhaps you should love yourself enough to get rid of the unnecessary pain in your life. If they constantly disrespect you and you just live with it then they just might "love" you more than you love yourself. And *that's* the immediate problem.

Apr 22, 2015 7:20 AM

Although you're nervous about it and you don't know how it's going to turn out, you are a survivor. You've survived before and you'll survive again. The difficult thing is not letting the stress of the situation control you and make you mentally and physically sick while your troubles are once again eventually resolved. Controlling stress is easier said than done. But it *can* be done. Smile anyway.

Apr 23, 2015 6:30 AM

A jealous friend or family member can be more dangerous than a known enemy. Although you may not understand their jealousy...do not take it lightly. Secretly...they smile at your suffering and scoff at your efforts. Remember...the problem that they have with you is theirs...not yours.

Apr 23, 2015 7:46 PM

Don't let stress convince you that an unpleasant situation is permanent. Always remember to use tomorrow for what it's for, and that is hope. Feel that it will be okay and it will. Make conscious attempts to not allow stress to hide the fact that everything will work out. No matter what it is. Everything will be just fine. Eventually, it always is.

Apr 24, 2015 6:06 AM

Let's go! It's time to keep the promises you made to yourself yesterday. Good morning my friends.

Apr 29, 2015 6:53 AM

There are women in my family whose self-esteem is almost as low as their standards in men. They introduce pieces of shit into our family and expect everyone else to just "deal with it". I will *never* understand their consistent attraction to rapists, crackheads, bums, child molesters, thieves, and just all around garbage. These are beautiful women who could easily be in a relationship with a "decent" guy but they *choose* to be with men who are or should be in jail. They know these men are garbage even from the beginning but their standards are so low that it doesn't matter. They bring this garbage around their children and in some cases they even have children with these pieces of shit. It's so sad that we as a family are always forced to deal with these ladies' terrible decisions. Perhaps they should find out what "self-worth" means. And then go acquire some. I mean damn, when does it end?

Apr 30, 2015 5:41 AM

You don't *have* to let someone else's problems become yours. Some people are just addicted to drama and negativity. Let them handle their own self-inflicted problems while you continue on your journey towards happiness and peace. Let no one and nothing obscure your focus or ruin your motivation.

May 02, 2015 9:37 AM

Choose to be alright and you will be. Negative feelings, no matter how powerful they are, must be controlled, eased from your mind and forcibly replaced with facts. Facts like, "I'm going to be alright no matter what". I *know* this can be done for I do it daily. Good morning my friends.

May 03, 2015 6:50 AM

This is how I'm feeling this beautiful morning, today would have been my beloved mother's 67th birthday. I'm off of work so I'll spend this day reminiscing all alone. My thoughts will make me cry sometimes and they will make me smile sometimes. Either way, today my heart and my time belong to my mother. I will be alone today. I really miss her. Good morning my friends.

May 04, 2015 8:52 AM

Stay focused and keep fighting!!! These "problems" aren't stronger than us. The only reason we want to give up is because we're tired. Our beating hearts are proof that we still have fight left in us. We won't waste it. We will let *nothing* convince us that it's over and we've lost. We will keep swinging until our damn arms fall off and then we will start kicking. God gives unlimited strength and man gives us unlimited doubt. Who are we going to listen to?

May 06, 2015 8:02 AM

I can't help you. In fact, no one can. Sometimes you just have to look in the mirror for help. Sometimes what needs to be done can only be done by you and you alone. Although "help" is always welcomed, it is not always available or useful. When I fall and no one is there to help me up, I stand up on my own. I sometimes stand up with tears in my eyes, with doubt surrounding me, with my shoulders stacked with heavy problems but I still stand up and move. I know that I am not finished. My brain is still functioning and my heart is still beating. I still have life. As long as you have "life", you have a chance. And as long as you have a chance, giving up is not an option. Life is not *all* about "standing up" a lot of times it requires "getting up". Even if you have to do it all alone. We may not be rich or highly educated, but we are warriors. The "struggle" has made warriors of you and me. Just believe it and it will be true. Good morning my friends.

May 06, 2015 10:54 AM

We all go through "changes". Those of us who resist the "change" suffer longer. Embrace it and move on. The book of life has many pages. Sometimes relief is just a page or two away. Keep turning. It's not over.

May 10, 2015 5:58 AM

Happy Mother's Day. I would like to say it to you specifically. You awoke this morning like you do almost every morning. Wondering how. Wondering how you got through yesterday, and with today not showing any signs of being different than yesterday, you're wondering how are you going to do it again. Almost immediately you are besieged by the "needs of children". No matter how you feel. Sick, angry, tired, overwhelmed with worry, you *must* deal with this. You must deal with it with patience and unbelievable control. I don't know how you do it day in and day out. You have no choice because your shoulders alone bare the weight and stress that comes along with "the needs of children" and all that it entails. You are a single mother. I want to say a very special Happy Mother's Day to you specific ladies. I know it can be hard to see the future with the present being so overwhelming but I promise you that one day your many sacrifices will pay off. One day your heart and mind will be able to relax and you will feel accomplished. Until then, your children need you and more importantly, they *have* you. May this Mother's Day be filled with joy for you...the single mother.

May 14, 2015 7:16 AM

Some people blame their parents for the struggles in their own life. I used to do that. I used to go around saying, "My own bad decisions have to be someone else's fault." As silly as that sounds, I truly believed it. The older I get, the more I realize, this brain is mine. And the decisions that come out of it are all mine. Be they good or bad, they're mine. They always have been and they always will be.

Blaming others for your own bad decisions is a lame attempt to separate yourself from the responsibility of your own life. That doesn't work for me nor against me.

May 15, 2015 9:56 AM

Yep, it's time to practice what I preach. A particular situation is trying to make me, once again, worry for nothing. Stress is trying to slowly creep into my life. But I look ahead and I see a resolution. No amount of stress or worrying can make me blind to the fact that everything will be alright. Instead of keeping this fact on the backburner, I will bring it to the forefront of my psyche and I will put the stress and worry on the backburner and keep my focus on the inevitable resolution of this situation. I feel how I *want* to feel. No outside source will dictate whether I'm content or not. None. My happiness comes from the inside out, very rarely from the outside in. I do not adapt to situations; I make situations adapt to me. Every new day, I allow the pristine nature of my aura to consume my personality. With it, I smile and help others without a second thought to what I have put on the "backburner". No unpleasant situation can disrupt that. I feel how I *want* to feel. I control me in *every* way.

May 17, 2015 11:51 AM

I commend single ladies with no man who know their worth and won't just settle for any so called man. They would rather be alone than to compromise their character. You ladies are my heroes. Stay on your pedestal and let *no* man pull you off of it. The right man would rather join you than change you.

May 19, 2015 11:57 AM

Weakness is a chosen trait. You're only as weak as you personally think you are. Nobody said life was going to be easy. It's time to show *everybody* what you're made of. Stand up and man up. Strength or weakness. It's *your* choice. There is *nothing* you can't overcome, but only if you believe it. This is not the time to just sit around feeling sorry for yourself. This is the time to find that second wind, that strength within, now get your ass up and let's begin!

May 20, 2015 7:00 AM

Those who doubt you are merely saying that they themselves couldn't do it. Only doubting yourself has any real meaning.

May 22, 2015 7:27 AM

You cannot and will not lead with words alone. You lead by example. Actions not only speak louder than words but they are more memorable too. While children can hear what you say, they are much more apt to do what you do.

May 23, 2015 7:13 AM

Yesterday I found out that there are actually folks out here who don't like me. Well, I hope it's not my smile that they dislike because I'll be giving out healthy doses of that today. I feel good today. I'm sorry to those who were hoping for something different. Good morning my friends.

May 23, 2015 1:10 PM

Sadly...some people are so unhappy that they absolutely hate the happiness of others. They doubt it and call it "phony". Phony? Perhaps. But I'd rather fill my heart with "phony" happiness than genuine bitterness any day. We're over here surrounded by happiness. You can either join us or sit back and envy us. Either way, we're smiling so hard that it hurts our cheeks a little.

May 25, 2015 9:34 AM

Does he stay out all night with basically no explanation? Does he hit you at all? Does he degrade your accomplishments and doubt your efforts? Does he disrespect your children and/or your parents? Does he not want you to have any friends? Does he control your phone? Does he hide his phone? Is he too lazy and uninterested to work and provide financial stability? Does he take your money? Does he call you demeaning names more than he calls you by the name your mother gave you? Does he disrespect you daily for no other reason than because he can? Does he set bad examples for your children?

My friend, life is too short to answer "yes" to *any* of those questions. He has made you feel so ugly. What has he done in his life that would warrant you letting such a man make you feel that way? I suspect the answer is "not a damn thing". Quit wasting time waiting on him to change and begin to change yourself. Do it today. Do it now. You're beautiful. Remind yourself of that today.

Some of you dudes might be saying, "Why is Clyde hating and why does he care how we treat these girls?"

Well, I know from personal experience that it takes a weak man to bully a woman who he professes love. And also, I've got a daughter you weak bitch.

May 26, 2015 9:23 AM

There are a ton of things in life that are completely out of our control. Fortunately for us, our attitude towards others isn't one of them. A bad or a good attitude is a choice. Control your choice. And if you choose to have an unpleasant attitude, be prepared to deal with the unpleasant consequences.

May 28, 2015 6:38 PM

Whatever produces a genuine, healthy smile, I'm all about that.

May 30, 2015 8:38 AM (MF)

I'm thinking about my grandfather (my mother's father) this morning. I remember when I was 11 and he was at our house talking about football. He said the Dolphins played the Jets in a Super Bowl. Even at 11 I knew that had never happened before and so I told him as much. He began to let me know how wrong and stupid I was. I had a chrome bike that I had built from the ground up because my mother could never buy me one. My grandfather looked at my beautiful bike sitting in the hallway and said, "I'll bet you $50 against your bike that the Dolphins played the Jets in a Super Bowl." Of course I said, "okay". Back then there were no cell phones or computers so my mother spent a while calling radio stations and TV stations to prove who was right. After it was proven, he gave me $50. I was an 11-year-old dirt poor kid with $50. I was ecstatic. After he gave me the money he said to me, "I'll play you in some cards for that money." Now I had never really played cards against an adult before. I had watched the adults play and practiced with my siblings but I was 11 years old and knew almost nothing about what I was about to do. I looked at my mother and she gave me no indication on whether I should do this or not. For some reason, she respected this man, who had abused her and her sisters practically their whole lives. We sat down at the table and began to gamble for the money I had just won off of him. Needless to say, he made short work of me. He took all of his money back and quickly. After he took the money back, he gave me another offer. This time he would play me for my beloved bike. With the feeling of having $50 a half an hour ago still fresh in my mind, I agreed. My grandfather won my bike from me. I tried to act like a man about it, but I wasn't a man, I was an 11-year-old kid. I cried as he put my bike in his trunk. My mother just watched him and said nothing. I watched him leave with my bike in his trunk. For a minute, I actually thought he would bring it back. I actually thought he was a human being. He never brought it back. One day I overheard one of my aunts tell my mother that he had given it to my cousin. My mom's racist sister's son.

My grandfather died in the 90's so he's been in Hell for a while now. He was a racist pedophile. I doubt he even knew my real name. I think he thought it was "Lil Nigger". He couldn't have cared less about his black grandchildren and he had no problem letting us know this right to our faces.

I'm thinking about you this morning Grandpa. And now that I think about it, I realize something, I realize that I forgive you. No matter what kind of monster you chose to be, without you, there is no me.

May 31, 2015 12:12 PM

I'm having a bad day. But that's okay because I still have a good life, so I smile.

Jun 05, 2015 8:24 AM

It was a rough day yesterday for us. A wasted day perhaps. The house was full of disagreements and vitriol. But that was yesterday. We've moved on. That's how we've made it work for so long. We consciously recognize an argument for what it is, temporary. Very temporary.

Jun 09, 2015 2:44 PM

My shoulders are so strong. I carry my "problems" alone. All alone. It makes me so proud of myself to know that I need not one soul to move forward. I'm not saying that others wouldn't be there for me if I needed them to but I don't need it. My shoulders are strong. I don't need support. At least not right now. I feel good about that.

Jun 11, 2015 11:43 AM

You should expect what you've earned, be it good or bad. So many people want what they don't deserve and yet they don't want what they do deserve.

Jun 13, 2015 5:10 PM

I love it when I kick the odds in the fuckin face.

Jun 14, 2015 9:20 AM

I just want to be happy. *Correction*, I'm just *going* to be happy. Whatever and whomever attempts to stand in the way of my mission will be dealt with accordingly.

Jun 16, 2015 5:44 PM

Don't you worry Baby Girl...I got you

You ain't 'bout to slip at all

As long as I got breath in my body...

You'll *never* slip...let alone fall

Jul 03, 2015 11:02 AM

Father Time...you old sly dog you. Why don't I care to listen to my car's stereo loudly anymore? When the hell did I get all of this patience? Me and "waiting" never got along before but now we're becoming really good friends. Father Time...I am conscious of you changing me. Let's not do anything too drastic too soon. Be nice Father Time...be nice.

Jul 06, 2015 6:50 AM

I truly hate feeling sorry for people. I feel so compelled to help them even though I cannot. Sometimes mere words of encouragement just aren't enough. Sometimes we must turn and walk away from the situation with a heavy heart. Sometimes we must cut ties with someone who is only interested in being a self-destructive emotional burden. Sometimes, there's just nothing else you can do.

Jul 06, 2015 11:25 AM

I think I saw her suffering all the time. However, she would rarely let on that she was in fact suffering. She hated her life but I only know this because I think she *should* have hated it. She never gave me any real hint of the depression that her chosen path must have placed upon her psyche. She was a smart woman who, for whatever reason, was incapable of leading her own life. She needed a leader. Unfortunately for her, the men, and in some cases, women, she chose to let lead her weren't going anywhere positive. She spent years just running in place. Then she ran out of motivation to run so she just stood there for several more years. After a while, her desire to even stand began to wane so she laid down. Sadly, she would never get back up. Honestly, she never even tried to get back up. Over time, I watched great potential be wasted right before my eyes. In the end, I knew that I had been watching someone I love slowly but surely give up in life. In the end, I knew she was just hanging around waiting to die. I could see it yet I was helpless to prevent it.

Why? Why did she do this? What was preventing her from realizing that she had so much more to offer, so much more to do? Why did she *never* see that?

It is indeed a cycle. A preventable cycle, but a cycle nonetheless. I watched her stand with her hands at her side while life just beat the hell out of her. She did almost nothing to fight back.

And now...now I am watching her offspring do the same thing that she did. Even worse.

God...

I know you've given me more weapons against this cycle than just these useless tears. I need your help. Just like with my mother, I'm lost and I don't know what to do except close my eyes and ask for help. Help us Dear Lord, help us help her.

Jul 14, 2015 6:09 AM

You don't always need to receive an apology to forgive someone. Forgiving someone is more about your own peace of mind.

Jul 15, 2015 8:39 AM

It is a fact that even major problems are so easy to deal with when they belong to someone else. It's easy to question someone else's decision even if we know in our hearts that we might have made the exact same decision given the circumstances. Only a perfect person can see a situation that they *could* truly *never* find themselves in.

It's so easy to judge and say, "Look at you." "Look at this mess you've made." Forgetting that our time to be judged could be right around the corner. Only a perfect person never makes a mess. And since there aren't any perfect people, be careful with the judging.

Jul 24, 2015 3:45 AM

Y'all want to be out here trying to take shortcuts, selling drugs and shit and then when they pop your ass and you go to jail, you want to start blaming your family for "ignoring" you. You can either struggle to make ends meet *with* your freedom or you can try to take shortcuts and end up struggling *without* your freedom. Either way, the choice is completely *yours*. And so are the consequences. Don't try to make someone else lay in a bed that *you* chose to make. I'm sorry but life is not as easy as you want it to be. How much effort you're willing to put into it directly determines what you're going to get out of it. It's just the way it is. THERE ARE NO SHORTCUTS!

Jul 25, 2015 6:03 AM

I touch lives almost daily. Mostly with just a kind yet sincere word. Sometimes with a kind yet sincere act. Sometimes I'm just an ear to someone who needs me to listen to them. Sometimes they want my advice or opinion, which I'm more than willing to give on almost any subject. I love doing all those things.

According to my "Quit Smoking" app, I've added 5 days back onto my life so far by quitting smoking. That's 5 more days that I get to do what I love to do. That's 5 more days, and counting.

Jul 28, 2015 8:38 AM

I think you should have some sympathy for those sad souls who consistently lash out at others because they don't know how to lash out at themselves. Keep in mind that it's hard to blame ourselves. Even when it's obvious that any perceived blame should be placed right upon our very own shoulders.

Aug 02, 2015 5:49 AM

As my late, beautiful mother would always say, "You got any money?"

Aug 02, 2015 5:53 AM

My wife has talked me into getting a second cat when I was supposed to be talking her into getting rid of the first one. It's some crazy cat lady Jedi mind trick shit that happened to me.

Aug 02, 2015 5:57 AM

I don't like conflict. Conflict always makes me feel as if I'm going to take this shit way too far.

Aug 02, 2015 6:09 AM

My compassion is somewhat limited and I'm alright with that.

Aug 04, 2015 4:21 PM

Sometimes people hate you because they envy you and you don't even realize how they feel until it's too late.

Aug 06, 2015 1:17 PM

Debt Collectors...

If I didn't pay the people who hired you, what the hell makes you think you have a chance? I don't even owe *you*. I owe *them*. Let them fight their own fuckin battles. Debt Collectors...I have no beef with you.

Aug 07, 2015 9:25 AM

I don't give a damn what happens, I've been overcoming my whole life. I'm built, inside and out, to overcome *anything*. You are too.

Aug 10, 2015 6:32 AM

You see, the thing is, it is not the end of the world. It's not even the end of *your* world. Perhaps it's time to show even yourself what you're made of. Until you have not one breath left...try. Try because you can. Try because you simply must.

Aug 11, 2015 6:27 AM

Sometimes I find it very hard to accept this as my fate. Unfortunately for me, I was not blessed with ignorance. I am a firm believer in ignorance being bliss. The opposite of ignorance is knowledge. They say knowledge is power. I would much rather have bliss than power. My bliss is limited by my knowledge and my power is limited by my effort and opportunity.

My point is, I *know*, and I wish I didn't.

Aug 21, 2015 5:18 PM

Sorry but I don't do negative. Unless it's funny. If it's negative and *not* funny, sorry, I don't do it.

Aug 25, 2015 7:36 AM

This day has started out rough. I *almost* smoked but I will not let one day of turmoil ruin even one of my goals. Everything will be fine. I will let time work it out for me like always. Just breathe, Clyde. Calm down and focus on the long term.

Done.

Now we're moving forward.

Aug 26, 2015 6:55 AM

For *anyone* whom I've *ever* known, if you think I'm angry with you or that I'm holding a grudge against you, you're wrong. And if you're angry with me and holding a grudge against me, and you think I care, then you're wrong again.

Aug 28, 2015 10:48 AM

If you take your past and embrace it and confess it and proclaim change and prove it, it will be impossible for anyone to use your past against you. No matter what it entails.

Aug 30, 2015 7:03 AM

Let them call you names, let them judge you, let them lie on you, let them hate. After all, it's the *only* power they have. It's completely up to *you* whether it works on you or not.

Aug 30, 2015 8:34 AM

Of course there are problems and obstacles. Without them we would have no scale to know just how strong we truly are. Think about what you've already made it through *All* the stuff you thought you wouldn't make it through and now it is behind you. Remember that?

Aug 30, 2015 9:03 AM

You can deny the truth from now until the end of time. It will matter very little to the truth. The truth cannot be denied. It can only be ignored. Especially when dealing with your own self.

Sep 01, 2015 6:18 AM

I awoke this morning dead tired. I made my coffee and promptly spilled it all over the floor. I got in my car to leave for work and the car wouldn't go into gear. Finally got it into gear and then I back out the garage and I run over a huge plant pot "someone" put in the middle of the driveway.

This day owes me for the way it started and I expect to be paid with a *fantastic* day!

Sep 02, 2015 9:34 AM

I may be kind of weird, but I love it when a woman has a potty mouth. Especially when I don't expect it. Not "sexually" dirty but just "cuss word" dirty.

Sep 04, 2015 8:16 AM

If you personally know in your heart that you gave it your very best, then failure becomes irrelevant.

Sep 05, 2015 5:22 AM

I just have a 5 AM feeling that today is going to be a *great* day! I'm feeling good and Sherri is feeling good. I hope no one has a bad attitude around me today because I'm probably going to be pissing you off. But I'm not doing it on purpose. I just want to love my life.

Sep 05, 2015 4:57 PM

It is very possible to be a nice person *and* demand respect. It's all about how you carry yourself.

Sep 12, 2015 8:14 AM

I will *never* stop trying to be a better, happier person. I've spent way more than enough of my life being miserable. I understand that some of us are just "happier" being miserable. And that's okay. I just prefer to go in a different direction.

Sep 15, 2015 3:44 AM

Perhaps it is time to put down the excuses and pick up a purpose. Trust me, you can't hold both.

Sep 18, 2015 10:31 AM

I don't need organized religion to have a good relationship with GOD. GOD has proven that to me my whole life.

Sep 19, 2015 10:58 AM

I don't put "fake smiles" upon my face. My positive attitude is from the heart. If it wasn't from my heart, then why would my positive attitude even exist? I've seen and lived the opposite of what I want to be *and* what I want to do with myself as a person. I've treated people the opposite of how I should have treated them and because of that, I have amends to make.

CONTROL...that's what it's all about. Complete *control* of my own mind, body, behavior and decisions. I am currently more at peace with myself than I've ever been in my life. I'm at a place that I *never* thought I could *ever* get to mentally. *I've still got a lot of work to do*, but I'm moving forward with my life. I just want to be happy *No matter what.*

ALSO...

For those of you who believe in me, and there are plenty of you, thank you so much.

AND...

For those of you who doubt me, and there are plenty of you, stay tuned...

Sep 24, 2015 10:18 AM

You'll be fine. These problems are temporary. Never underestimate the word *temporary*. More importantly, never mistake it for permanent.

You'll be fine. *No matter what,* you'll be fine. Don't continually prove to yourself how strong you are and yet continually doubt your strength. Believe in it, especially when temporary problems need handled. You'll be fine.

Sep 26, 2015 5:54 AM

I love good, positive, supportive people. Although it may not seem like it in a world where negativity is personified, there are a *whole lot* of good, positive, supportive people everywhere. I love to help people and stand up for people. I love to put a genuine smile on someone's face or relieve their stress with an act or word of kindness. All I want to do is see you succeed and be happy and if I can help you achieve that then, please, don't hesitate to ask. Nothing pleases me more than watching someone beat the odds and implement real happiness into their life. I don't care who you are or how you feel about me, I swear, I just want you to be happy. Happiness breeds happiness.

Sep 27, 2015 6:56 AM

INSECURITY

Insecurity: uncertainty or anxiety about oneself; lack of confidence

Insecurities: in the long run you will wonder why you cared about them.

Insecurities: "Stop signs" when there are no crossroads.

Insecurities: will make you feel like every single person on earth is a stranger

Insecurities: will make you ask "why me" instead of "why not me".

Insecurities: *everybody* has them. Not just you. The difference is the power given to them.

Believe in yourself every day. Believe that *you* are special. You'll soon find out how right you truly are. But it starts with belief.

Sep 29, 2015 10:48 AM

If you've ever questioned whether human beings have souls or not, then you've never been depressed. Because in your soul is where the pain from depression radiates from. I've been there my friend. When I was younger there was a time or two in my life that I sat on the edge of my bed with my pistol in my hand, tears in my eyes, and my heart so heavy that I could barely stand up. I was convinced that this was the only way to stop the constant pain and sorrow from torturing me any longer. A few times I have put my gun to my head and cocked the hammer, ready to end the pain, to end the misery that seemed to catch up with me no matter how fast I ran from it. Not once did *anyone* who loves me enter my mind. Not once did I say, "Tomorrow is a new day, a new beginning." Depression has nothing to do with a "beginning". It's all about "ending". Ending the pain and embarrassment that comes with disliking everything about myself. I never wanted anyone to feel sorry for me so I tried my best to keep the way I was feeling to myself. I would close my eyes, put the gun to my head, and with tears running down my face I would scream at the top of my lungs. After I would realize that I didn't do it, all of the emotional energy that I had just used would cause me to collapse and become a sobbing mess curled up on the floor begging God to *"PLEASE HELP ME"*. Asking God what he wants from me. Pleading for him to "just let me go". Oh, I've been there my friend. More than once. And although I pray that I never go back, I realize that having depressing thoughts is sometimes out of my control but how I handle those thoughts is completely within my control. I try to remain positive no matter what's going on with me. I do my best to stay away from negative situations and negative people. I'm happy *most* of the time and the times I'm not happy, you'll find me somewhere attempting to locate some positive happiness no matter where I get it from. Happiness for me comes from changing my life for the better. Treating people good, helping people, and watching people smile and be happy. That's what makes me happy. I stay happy simply because I choose to. And there was a time in my life when I didn't know that I had that choice.

Although depression is different for different people, I personally choose to handle it with genuine happiness. You can't fake genuine happiness. Just like you can feel the sadness from depression in your soul, you can also feel the elation from happiness in your soul. My soul is so filled with happiness right now that there is no room for any negativity at all.

Oct 04, 2015 7:37 AM

Perhaps you need to just calm down and focus. Panic and anger are *never* good things. Panic and anger are two things that we can control. Do away with the panic and anger and implement trust and realization. In other words, trust in the realization that no matter what life throws at you, it will work out. Whether it be by time, faith, or just plain human strength, it will work out. Don't exacerbate the situation with worry and stress. Worry and stress are the "bedbugs" of your brain. Exterminate them and they go away. Change the way you think so they never come back. Never stop practicing being under complete control of you mind, body, soul, actions and reactions. Perhaps practice doesn't truly make perfect, but it certainly makes it easier. Practice controlling what you always let control you. Panic, anger, worry and stress, how much they control you is up to you. I know this for sure. Tell yourself, "This is not the end of the world" and then truly realize how absolutely *true* that statement is, and then get to handling your business.

Oct 09, 2015 3:49 AM

Sometimes in life we have situations that upset us for whatever reason. Sometimes in life we wish we could change the way someone is behaving. Sometimes in life we wish we could help someone who is struggling with something but doesn't deserve to be struggling.

Sometimes in life, *all* we can do about something is care.

And sometimes that's just the way it is.

Oct 22, 2015 6:35 AM

Your focus is always under attack by doubters and the jealous. They don't want you to focus. They want you upset and doubting yourself just like they themselves do daily. Don't fall for it. Let no person, nor object, nor situation ruin your focus. This is a brand new day. This is the fresh start that God gives each of us daily. Focus.

Oct 22, 2015 3:29 PM

Sherri: I think I'm pregnant.

Me: Yeah right.

Sherri: No, for real.

Me: Why are you saying that?

Sherri: Look how my belly is growing.

Me: You can't get pregnant by potato chips.

Oct 26, 2015 6:41 AM

Give your child all of the time that they need from you while they are children. If you don't, I promise you, you'll regret it. When they are old enough to hold you accountable, an apology will not do you any good. They won't care about your excuses nor your regret nor your tears. I know this from experience. All I can do now is sit here and say, "If only I had it to do all over again". And those words mean absolutely *nothing* to anyone.

If you rarely see your child, change it now because it will be all but impossible to change it later. Fix it now before it leads to emotional torture that you will deserve.

Nov 05, 2015 9:55 AM

Back in January of 2011 I quit smoking. I lasted 152 days. After 152 days I let the "stress" of a day get to me and I began smoking again on the 152nd day. It was the longest I had gone without smoking since I began smoking back in 1987.

In June of 2015 (this year) I quit smoking again. Today is a special day to me because today is day 153. I am officially one day ahead of where I was the last time I attempted to rid myself of this vile vice. I feel stronger than ever about moving forward with cigarettes being merely a bad part of my past that has no place in my future. It has not been easy but it is certainly getting easier. I feel so good and I can't help but tell you about it!!!!!!

Nov 12, 2015 6:06 AM

We all have problems not just you. Everything that you're going through, we all go through it too. So you see, what's going on with you is nothing new.

Chin up, focus, now go do what you have to do.

Nov 17, 2015 5:22 AM

Negativity is not a cold. Just because someone else has it doesn't mean *you* have to catch it from them no matter how close to them you are. Let them be negative while you count and appreciate your blessings. Negative words are easy to ignore. *STAY POSITIVE.*

Nov 20, 2015 10:31 AM

I very rarely comment about politics or religion and I will not do it now. However, what's happening in our world right now isn't just about politics or religion. I have a Syrian friend and all she is, is a woman who is afraid for her loved ones. She is hurting and sick with worry like anyone would be. I truly understand how some of you feel. Terrorists are murderers. That's all they really are. Just like not every black person is a criminal and just like not every white person is a racist and just like not every Asian eats dogs and just like not every German is Anti-

Semitic, etc., not every Syrian is a terrorist. I get it that some of you couldn't care less about showing a little compassion toward someone that you merely perceive as a threat, but for me, *I WILL NOT JUDGE EVERY PERSON WITHIN A GROUP OF PEOPLE BY THE ACTIONS OF A FEW.* I wouldn't want anyone doing that to me or to you. I understand that the world is a scary place right now. But don't let these animals make you compromise your decency as a human being *and* as an American. I have read some of your words and it just breaks my heart that there are folks like my Syrian friend reading that hateful stuff while their hearts weigh heavy with a kind of worry that most of us couldn't even imagine. I pray for every single innocent, decent person and animal on this planet. I wish us *all* peace, health and happiness. No matter your race, sexual orientation, gender, handicap, or ethnicity, if you are a decent person, I have nothing but compassion for you. Let us *all* pray for every single innocent, decent person just trying to do right by their family and be as happy as they can be on earth today. *Every single person.*

Nov 29, 2015 6:31 AM

I awoke this morning feeling a little down in the dumps. I'm missing people who aren't here anymore and I'm wishing I could do more for my loved ones who need help. Tis the season, I suppose. I laid in my bed when I first woke up this morning staring into the darkness thinking about these particular people. I cried a little and I prayed a little.

I know that *all* I am capable of giving is "my best" and that's what I'm going to give you every single day, *my best*. Whether it's advice, money or time, if I have it, and you need it, it's yours. If I possess what it will take to make you smile again then prepare to smile again. I will not judge you. I will only love you. Let's smile and laugh together because that's what I love doing with my life.

Dec 03, 2015 3:38 AM

Sometimes life is hard and it seems unfair for us. Sometimes it forces us to stand on our *own* two feet and when it does, so be it. Let's do this!

Dec 10, 2015 5:34 AM

TIME:

It's what I use when things are rough. Sometimes I need to remind myself to let it work. Sometimes I need to remind myself how blessed I truly am. And so are you.

Dec 23, 2015 4:53 AM

Life is so very tough right now for me. I ask my wife what can I do, she points up.

UP... it's where I'm locating guidance and strength to pull through these *very* trying times.

God is *always* good. AMEN?

Dec 26, 2015 10:12 PM

If you let someone control you merely with negative words, then essentially you're giving control to whomever wants it.

In other words, fuck what they say.

Dec 27, 2015 8:37 AM

Sometimes I think about the fact that I've come a long way when it comes to improving my self-control. And then something happens that reminds me that I still have a long way to go.

I'm still a work in progress. Please be patient.

<u>2016</u>

Jan 01, 2016 7:57 AM

I cannot look a wrong man in his eye and tell him that he is right. I refuse to do that. No matter what it costs me.

Jan 04, 2016 7:12 AM

Just in case you didn't know it, I'm not perfect. I'm not even all that "good". I'm coming from a place where the road is now paved with my "forgiveness requests".

I've got so far to go and when I finally get to where I need to be, I pray that the people who truly love me are right there offering me any forgiveness that I may need.

As I've gotten older, I've truly come to understand the power in saying, "I'm sorry" and *truly* meaning it.

If I need it from you then I request it from you...

Please forgive me if you can.

Jan 05, 2016 2:36 PM

So what...?

It's not the end of the world.

Tomorrow's a new day.

Collect the lesson and move on.

...and that goes for pretty much anything.

Jan 18, 2016 2:25 PM

He didn't have to do it. I never even hinted to him that he should do it.

Today, while I was at work a coworker came up to me and we exchanged pleasantries along with the usual banter him and I exchange regularly. As we were talking, I noticed he had $20 in his hand. I thought it was kind of strange. I mean, he didn't owe me any money and he certainly hadn't bought anything off of me. After we were done with our "hello's" he reached toward me to hand me the $20. Of course I'm confused so I give him the "what's this for" look. He said, "It's for your brother." I immediately felt a lump in my throat and I felt as though I could tear up but I wasn't going to let that happen, not here, not now. I thought about handing it back to him but I didn't want to seem ungrateful because believe me, *I was not* ungrateful. I shook his hand and thanked him wholeheartedly. I told him that he had no idea how much his caring act meant to me. It wasn't necessarily the money as much as it was the thought.

This is significant for a couple of reasons...

First of all, I think I can safely say that neither one of us is going to get rich doing what we do so *any* money is "important money". Every dollar counts.

Secondly, he didn't have to do it. He cared and I didn't even know he did. I mean, I knew he probably didn't hate me but I never thought he would give my personal troubles a second thought. I've never really discussed my brother with him. At least I can't remember doing that. Perhaps he read about it. Either way, this made me realize that sometimes people are thinking about your problems with you and you may not even know it. You're on someone's mind because you are troubled in some way. Someone cares. Even if you think that no one does. You should know that someone does. Someone cares about what you're going through and they wish they could help you. We all provide each other with hope when we need it. As long as we have hope, we have reason. Sometimes God sends one of our fellow human beings to let us know that we should never feel abandoned. And that it is *impossible* for God to abandon us.

Thank you my friend. God bless you and all of us.

Jan 30, 2016 5:18 AM

Let me tell you about my homeboy though. He just always comes through for me while asking for almost nothing. You know that person in your life that you would try to run through a brick wall for...? Yeah, well, that's my homeboy to me. My homeboy calls me every day. Literally. Out of everybody in my family, I only see my wife more than I see my homeboy. Even though I already know, my homeboy lets me know every day how much I mean to him. Sometimes that thought gets me through some tough situations. You see, me and my homeboy, we're tight like that. I'm calling him my "homeboy" but in reality, he is much more than a mere slang word to me. He is my son and he is my best friend. He is Clyde McCrae III.

Feb 03, 2016 7:55 AM

My mind tried to get me to worry about something a few minutes ago. We had a conversation. We went back and forth. My mind telling me why I should worry, and me telling my mind why worry is *only* harmful and useless. I brought up old times when we worried about something until we were damn near sick from worry and things just worked out anyway. My mind couldn't bring up not one time when our worry was warranted and we actually should have been worried. We've lived through every single thing that has happened to us so far, whether we worried about it or not. So, I think my mind understands now. We ain't worried about nothing. It is what it is. We're just living our life.

Feb 5, 2016 2:11 AM

We're so flawed, me and her. We argue about stupid stuff. She never just "lets it be my way". She has her own opinion and she very often uses it. We're different in so many ways. I love sports, she doesn't. She loves feral cats, I don't. When I say "yes" she will most likely say "no". Just to name a few of the many differences. There is no one in my life who is more honest with me than she is. She won't hesitate to humble me when I need to be humbled. I will admit, sometimes we don't like each other. That's right, sometimes *WE DON'T LIKE EACH OTHER*. You may be able to find us not liking each other if you try really hard to find it. But try as you might, you will *never* find us not loving each other. You will *never* find us not forgiving each other. You will *never* find us trying to hurt each other. You will *never* find us not doing whatever it takes to make our marriage work and to be happy with each other. I know for a fact that she is the very last woman on earth that I will ever lie down with, need, or give the ability to break my heart. At this point in my life, being loved and taken care of by her is like breathing to me, sometimes I don't even notice that it's happening until something tries to disrupt it. I just expect it. I love her and she loves me. And as long as that statement remains true, there isn't much that I can't get through. Happy Anniversary Mrs. Sherri McCrae.

Feb 17, 2016 8:09 AM

All you can do is try again.

If you make a mistake or have a lapse in judgement or fail at something, then there's   not much you can do about it other than try to do better next time.

There will be a next time. Life is all about "next times".

You must ignore those who will try to make you dwell on a mistake.

You must ignore the people who will pretend as though they're perfect.

Remember, they're just pretending.

They're judging you because it is much easier than judging themselves.

Period. Believe in yourself. You'll be fine.

Feb 20, 2016 11:10 AM

I love when the weather is nice. It always helps me renew my purpose.

Mar 02, 2016 9:39 AM

Teardrops.

We cannot truly know how someone is feeling inside because the heart does not have a window to peek into. I suppose God created the teardrop to show the outside world how you are feeling inside. The teardrop says so much. For me, I was not given the ability to hide my teardrops when they are ready to show themselves. When my heart is hurting, it forces me to show teardrops to the world. Embarrassing teardrops. Teardrops are the blood from the open wound that those whom I love are digging into with their actions. I see them hurting. I see their desperation. Their selfishness. Their complete foolishness. I understand it completely. The pressure upon my emotions is great right now. I cannot pull my loved ones up with me because my own weight is already so very heavy. I can barely lift it. When my mind's eye allows the plights of the ones I love to enter my heart, my heart bleeds teardrops that flow down my cheeks as clear, salty water. There's nothing I can do. There's nothing I can say to make it better or to make it stop. No words that I am aware of will work. No actions that I am capable of will work. My mind won't let me shut my loved ones out. And as soon as my heart gets a hint that so many of my loved ones are in dire trouble... teardrops. Teardrops. They're all I have. They're all that I can offer. And they're useless. Although my heart has produced countless teardrops over the years, they've never ever fixed anything. I used to see them as a sign of weakness, at least I don't see them as that anymore. I now see them as a glaring sign of a need for change. A need for God. I know that only God can wipe my face when it is this wet. When my heart is bleeding, it is never for me. It is always for you. I wish your demons were not stronger than you because, right now, they obviously are. Right now, in my family, we are struggling to make "it" better while easily making "it" worse. I tell myself "not to care". Let them destroy themselves. There's nothing that I can do anyways. But I lie to myself. There is something that I can do. I can pray and I can hope. Perhaps to some, those two things mean nothing. But to me, prayer and hope is all I have. They give meaning to my teardrops. I love my family. And I will never stop believing in you. Even if you stop believing in yourself, I'll be here to let you know, as long as my heart produces teardrops, it knows there is hope. No matter what happens, I will *never* give up on you. My teardrops will constantly remind me that I still care. Prayers up.

Mar 13, 2016 6:58 AM

I hope this day brings you way more happiness than you even thought possible. Today, smile, laugh and forgive as much as you can. This brand new day is full of hope. Let's all take advantage of it. I feel so blessed because I awoke this morning with no enemies. I hate absolutely *no one*. I only have love, hope, and forgiveness in me today... because it's what I choose. I love when life forces me to acknowledge my blessings.

Apr 11, 2016 6:21 AM

I know from experience that sometimes in life you have to literally *force* yourself to do the right thing. If you can't force yourself to do the right thing, then you should stop making decisions until you grow up. Doing the right thing even when the wrong thing seems so much better is what grown-ups do daily. Bad decisions have consequences. Real, tangible consequences. I also know from experience that you can live in denial all you want, but reality *will not* be ignored for very long. And when reality comes calling, good luck running from it. When it's time to face your action's consequences, crying, hurting and remorse will mean almost nothing even though crying, hurting and remorse will be *all* you will have. Every single one of your decisions belong to *you*. Even the stupid ones. Be careful.

Apr 18, 2016 4:19 PM

I hate that I am a hypocrite sometimes.

I'm working on that.

The first step is acknowledgment.

First step...done.

Apr 19, 2016 2:01 PM

Dear Clyde Jr.,

If you refuse to live without it...

then don't bitch about it

Love Always,

Your Common Sense

Apr 21, 2016 3:17 PM

Death shows no favoritism. None.

Apr 21, 2016 4:48 PM

You see, I know I did not know Prince personally and I know he is just another celebrity who happened to die. But you see, the difference with me is this...

I've been listening to Prince since before I can remember. For a lot of my adolescent years all I listened to was Prince. There isn't a note on any of his albums that I don't know. Those notes went with me through a lot of stuff growing up. Those notes, although just music, gave me something to look forward to when I had nothing. All I had and all I wanted were those notes. They are forever in my mind. I feel like a significant part of my childhood died today. I can't help but to feel that way. The good thing about it is that I still have every one of those notes. And I can't listen to them loud enough or long enough. It sure makes me miss being a kid. I used to dress like Prince. He was my identity as a youth. Although he will never play another note, the ones he already gave us will be a very important part of my life until I join him.

RIP to the best musician who ever lived.

Apr 28, 2016 7:11 AM

As we go through life today dealing with our problems and heartaches that seem so huge, let's say a prayer for those who feel alone while dealing with their problems and heartaches. May we all realize that we are *never* truly alone. Look up with faith. Open your heart and mind and accept the loving grace that is there for each one of us.

With tears in my eyes this morning, I ask God to walk with me and those I love. I ask God to walk with us all. Amen.

May 02, 2016 5:17 AM

I wake up in the morning with my mind heavy with worry. I think about, "this needs paid" or "that needs paid" or "this loved one is going through that" or "this hurts" or "that hurts". After I get all that stuff together in my mind and before I leave my house, I put it in a nice big box and then I set it at God's doorstep. And then I go on with my day believing and knowing that it will all be taken care of. Maybe not when I think it should be, but I am learning patience. I am going where God wants me to go. And I'll get there when I'm supposed to. Perhaps some of us are strong enough to handle our heartaches and tribulations on our own...

I am not that strong.

That's why I give it up. God is so very good!

May 08, 2016 6:56 AM

'Happy Mother's Day! It has been 1,313 days since my mother passed away. That's 3 years, 7 months and 4 days since my heartache began. It's not a regular heartache. It should have subsided at least a little by now and it hasn't.

Almost every morning I wake up, it feels like I just lost my mother the day before. It's getting to where I'm starting to wonder if I've gone crazy and should be seeking help. I can't get over it. I miss her more now than I ever have before. I miss everything about her. I can't have any pictures of her visible in my house. I tried to watch a video with her in it once, I found out that's not the best thing for me to do. Years ago, I "interviewed" my mother on a cassette tape and I have that tape. I listened to that tape once since she has been gone and I found out that that is another act I don't want to do. I miss her terribly. I will die missing her. As selfish as it may sound, it is true that I wish I would have died before her. The world can be a very lonely place when your heart is this broken. I don't understand why I can't get past this. I'm afraid that I never will. I cry a lot because I need to talk to her. I need to let her know how much I love her and need her in my life. I need her to know how sorry I am that I never made her truly proud of me. I miss her. My mother was not perfect but she was beautiful. I try not to focus on her imperfections but I often dwell on the beauty that she had. I miss her terribly. Once again it is Mother's Day. My fourth one without her. Personally, I'm not too fond of Mother's Day these days. Actually, I'm not real fond of any day since 10-03-12. I've told myself that I just need to "man-up" and move on from this. I've told myself this is "weak" and "silly". But it doesn't matter what I say because at this point, it has no bearing on how I feel. In no way is this looking for sympathy for myself. I don't need sympathy, I have God. And together we are working my situation out. I'm working with His time. I'll get there, in time. It is *only* through faith and God that I will ever see her again. And of course, I will see her again. I must. This is about appreciation. It is about recognizing how absolutely important a mother is, not only on this day, but every day. It is about realizing more often that no one is here forever. It is about having as little regret as possible when life turns someone into only memories. Happy Mother's Day to each and every one of you wonderful ladies. I know that you aren't "perfect", but who is? I loved my "imperfect" mother dearly, and your children love you. HAPPY MOTHER'S DAY!!!!!!!!

May 25, 2016 5:01 AM

Dear GOD:

Lately, whenever I'm alone I feel lonely. I look up to "The One and Only" …

If it be Your will…may it be my way. Walk with me oh Lord…walk with me today.

Remind me with Your grace that I am far from alone. Never by myself…never on my own

Though my heart may get trampled and maybe tossed aside...

And though I may have come up short no matter how hard I tried...

I'll know You stand beside me. That's why I trust that I will never fall.

I give my demons to You Lord. I give them...one and all.

When my body aches and my tired mind feels like it's almost had enough...

When the Devil tells me, "Just give up. You know you're not that tough."

I close my mind to those evil words, for I know they're not true.

How can I possibly ignore what You've already gotten me through?

I am not a perfect man and I'll never claim to be.

You knew I wouldn't be perfect the day You created me.

You knew my life would be a little more difficult than perhaps the average man's.

But not so hard that I wouldn't be thankful that You made me who I am.

I've denounced You and made fun of You and still...You're always there.

I've given you a million reasons to disown me...yet You always care.

When my tribulations are so heavy that I feel they just might win...

I go down to my knees and every time, You pick me up again.

Dear Lord I am thankful...for this and so much more.

For all that You've done for me and for all You still have in store.

One more thing...

I have a personal request Dear Lord...and I hope that it's okay....

Hug my mother and let her know...that I miss her every day.

Let her know that when she died...I lost my best friend. Let her know how hard I'm trying to see her once again. Amen.

May 26, 2016 4:42 PM

Hello People...

Most people know me in one way or another. I mean, I'm pretty popular. Sometimes they love me and sometimes they hate me. It really doesn't matter to me how they feel about me because once they get to know me, I become almost irresistible to them. I trick them into thinking I love them more than anyone else ever has and they fall for it every time. I'm very good at that. Actually, I don't have to lie to people because I can make them do whatever I need them to do anyway. Sometimes their families talk down about me to them but I don't care about that. They can't compete with me. They don't offer what I offer. I know how to take over someone's mind and heart and make them love me even though they know how I feel about them. I talk directly to their brain and they eat up every word I say. I've got to admit, sometimes I tell obvious lies and still, they eat it up. Some may be shocked at what I'm saying but this is nothing new. I'm so irresistible that I don't even care if people see what I've done to someone else. They can have positive proof that I am a liar and a manipulator yet I will still take over. I'm a "beast" like that. Some people I affect worse than others and I don't care about that. I mean, here I am being more honest than I've ever been and even still, those who already know me will *still* love me tomorrow. Even though I'm confessing here and now that I have no feelings for anyone and I never will. I am truly irresistible. At least, people make me think I am. And all that matters is what I think. I don't deal in reality. Whatever I think, is the way it's going to be. Whatever I want is what they're going to do. It's crazy but some people have actually mustered up the strength to leave me alone. When people do that I still try to get them to love me again. I'll try until they die. I love to pretend. I pretend to be their only way out of dire situations. I pretend to be the only one who *truly* understands them. I can't believe they fall for that. Okay people, I am being as honest as I possibly can be but it is not out of compassion, it is completely out of arrogance. I am unstoppable. I love money! I need money! People know this and it doesn't matter. It is *very* important that they spend money on me. I've turned good girls into whores and I've turned talented men into heartless street hustlers. It doesn't matter because I need money. It is *all* about money with me. Even those who know me well know that I won't even go around them without money. And they care about that. Well, I have lives to disrupt and destroy and I also have lies to tell and I also have people who are trying to resist me so I have to go kick a few butts. Thanks for reading this even though it will matter very little because as I've said before, I am irresistible. See you soon.

"Love" Always...ADDICTION.

Jun 5, 2016 5:11 AM

You see, at this point in my life, I just want peace. I don't want to argue and fight with anyone. I don't want to judge anyone or care about being judged by anyone. I just want peace. My mind and heart are tired from the Devil dragging me around for four and a half decades. Not only are they tired, but they are worn out and ready to shed any and all things and people that disrupt what I want. I just want peace. I hope I never have to yell at anyone again in my life. I hope I never have to throw my hands in anger again in my life. At this point in my life, I can comfortably walk away from any conflict, even if I haven't "won". That used to be all but impossible. It doesn't matter to me if I end up all by myself in a one-bedroom apartment eating cereal and watching old sit-coms every morning preparing to go to work. As long as I have a job and relatively good health and the occasional visit from those whom I love, I will be satisfied. Perhaps the "old" me is in the throes of death and a "new" me is slowly emerging. Whatever the case may be, I can feel God telling me that it is time. It is time for peace. And if it be God's will, may it be my way. You see, at this point in my life and moving forward, I don't want much. I just want peace.

Good Sunday morning and God Bless you my friends and famILY.

P.S. Today I am celebrating one full year of not smoking even one cigarette. I never thought that would ever be possible. I'm very proud of that.

June 19, 2016 2:50 PM

When I grew up, affection was rarely shown within our household. There was hardly any hugging and words like "I love you" certainly weren't being thrown around. Not by our mother and not by our father and not by each other. It was just the way it was. Unfortunately, when I became an adult, I let that carry on and I deprived my own children of the affection that I myself was deprived of. Although I love them more than anything in this world, I rarely told my children that I loved them. I rarely touched them with affection. It's not that I didn't want to, it was just that it didn't "feel" right at the time. Words like "I love you" and perhaps a "good morning hug" seemed like weakness to me because I was taught that it was weakness. I was "taught" wrong. For me, it's too late. I must suffer through knowing that my wonderful daughter will never have the affection from her father that she deserved as a little girl. My son's will never know what it feels like for their father to hug them and tell them how truly thankful I am for their existence. They're all grown now, never to be children again. You cannot rewind life. All you can do is say that you were wrong. I was so wrong. Because of this, my heart is full of regret. But when I see how my sons give their own children those feelings of love and affection that they themselves never really received from me, I think to myself, "at least it stopped with me". I want you all to know how much I truly love you and how incredibly proud of you I am. I want my baby girl to know that I accept any blame due for your heartache and your feelings of being 'lost' in this world. I'm so sorry. I will do my best to make it up to you with the time I have left on this earth. Happy Father's Day Clyde, Justin, Mike and Jordan. I promise that every time I see you for the rest of our lives, I will hug you and tell you that I love you. I know now that it's not a sign of weakness. It's a sign of how strong our bond truly should be. I love you. And although you're not a father yet, you too Anthony Confalone.

Jun 22, 2016 6:35pm

With the heavy weight of my own world on my own shoulders... I continue.

Alone... I move. Me, my thoughts and I... we are determined. Determined because there is nothing else.

God will not let me give up. Believe me, I've tried.

He has taken that part of my soul and put it somewhere that I am not.

Somewhere that I cannot find it anymore. I have no desire to stop. Even though I must do this alone... it must be done.

God's hand has slowly and steadily molded me and I've culminated to this...

I now know what I am capable of...

Perhaps more importantly...

I now know what I am NOT capable of...

and that is going backwards.

God is GOOD!